THE

EVERYTHING KIDS'

FOOTBALL BOOK

The all-time greats, legendary teams, today's superstars—
and tips on playing like a pro

Greg Jacobs, Reporter/Statistician, STATS, LLC

▲adamsmedia
Avon, Massachusetts

EDITORIAL
Director of Innovation: Paula Munier
Editorial Director: Laura M. Daly
Associate Copy Chief: Sheila Zwiebel
Acquisitions Editor: Kerry Smith
Development Editor: Elizabeth Kassab
Production Editor: Casey Ebert

PRODUCTION
Director of Manufacturing: Susan Beale
Production Project Manager: Michelle Roy Kelly
Prepress: Erick DaCosta, Matt LeBlanc
Interior Layout: Heather Barrett,
Colleen Cunningham

An Everything® Series Book.
Everything® and everything.com® are registered trademarks of F+W Media, Inc.

Published by Adams Media, a division of F+W Media, Inc.
57 Littlefield Street, Avon, MA 02322. U.S.A.
www.adamsmedia.com

ISBN 10: 1-59869-565-7
ISBN 13: 978-1-59869-565-6

Printed by R. R. Donnelley, Owensville, MO, USA.
January, 2010

10   9   8   7   6   5   4

This publication is designed to provide accurate and authoritative information with regard to the
subject matter covered. It is sold with the understanding that the publisher is not engaged in rendering
legal, accounting, or other professional advice. If legal advice or other expert assistance is required, the
services of a competent professional person should be sought.
—From a *Declaration of Principles* jointly adopted by a Committee of the
American Bar Association and a Committee of Publishers and Associations

Cover illustrations by Dana Regan
Interior illustrations by Kurt Dobler
Puzzles by Beth L. Blair

This book is available at quantity discounts for bulk purchases.
For information, please call 1-800-289-0963.

See the entire Everything® series at *www.everything.com.*

CONTENTS

The EVERYTHING KIDS' Football Book

Acknowledgments

I only get a few lines here, so I can't fully express my appreciation to all of these folks. But copious thanks anyway to: Bart and Mary Ann Jacobs, the late Jack Soete, Peter Cashwell, Clint Alexander, Keith Johnson, Gene Ware, David Glover, Brad "Spider" Caldwell, the Penn State football program, Andrea Bell, Kerry Smith, Grace Freedson. And, to my wife and sidekick Burrito Girl, a.k.a. Shari Jacobs, who lets me watch football on the big-screen TV all season. She's the best.

Dedication

To Milo Cebu, who at age four has demanded to learn
Woodberry's offensive playbook . . .

INTRODUCTION

Player. Coach. Fantasy team owner. Avid fan. There are so many ways to be involved in football. Whether you know a lot about football or hardly anything at all, this book has something to offer you.

If you're relatively new to football or if you're looking for new ways to play, Chapter 1 will answer all of your questions. Both long-time and new fans will enjoy the two chapters on professional football and the one on college football.

It is easy to find a high school game to watch locally or college and pro games on television. But for the players and coaches, the game itself represents the high point of weeks of preparation. It's not often that a telecast or newspaper report tells fans much about what goes on for a team before game day. But this book can help. Two chapters will give you some insight into the daily life of a team: Chapter 5, about high school football, tells you about life around the team. Chapter 9 talks about the people who make big contributions to the game behind the scenes. There is also advice on starting and running your very own fantasy football league.

If you've mastered the basics of football or want to learn more about the "X's and O's," there are two chapters to help you: one about offense and one about defense.

Hopefully, this book will be able to teach you something about football, no matter what you already know or don't know. Enjoy!

Where Did Football Come From?

In most countries other than the United States, when people talk about football they mean the game we call soccer. Here in the United States, football actually means football, as in the game you play with a brown, oval-shaped ball.

For most of history, people have played games with balls and goals. At least 500 years ago in England, the game we call soccer developed. In soccer, players try to put a round ball into a goal without using their hands.

In the early 1800s, players at the Rugby School in England started cheating. Instead of kicking the ball, they picked it up and ran with it into the goal. Some teams liked to play against the Rugby School—they just tackled whomever picked up the ball! Other teams wanted to play soccer the normal way. Soon two separate forms of the sport were played. In rugby, players were supposed to run with the ball, and defenders were supposed to tackle the ballcarrier to the ground.

Americans picked up the game of rugby, but every team wanted to play by different rules. In the late 1800s, several colleges and athletic clubs in America played games similar to rugby. East Coast schools such as Princeton, Rutgers, Harvard, and Yale eventually got together to try to standardize the rules.

By the turn of the century, American rugby had changed enough that you could probably have recognized the game as football. Every play was a running play. Blockers (without much padding) slammed into each other as hard as they could. There were so many injuries, in fact, that many people tried to ban the sport. At the personal request of President Teddy Roosevelt, Yale athletic director Walter Camp led a commission that created a more exciting and less dangerous game than had been played before. It was Camp who insisted that eleven players was the right number for a team. He invented the idea that the offense had to gain yardage to get a first down. Most importantly, Camp revolutionized football by inventing the forward pass.

The **EVERYTHING KIDS'** Football Book

College Football

College football in the early 1900s was dominated by the northeastern colleges that are now part of the Ivy League. In fact, it was 1912 before a non-Ivy League school won a national championship. College—not pro—football was the popular spectator sport through the first half of the 1900s. Colleges throughout the country formed teams, and more and more people started watching and playing football. The college bowl games on New Year's Day were the highlight of each season.

In the 1920s, colleges all over the country played football. Professional teams had started playing in the Midwest. Both the pro and college game were well known and well followed. However, football didn't become the big deal that it is now until after the Great Depression and World War II.

FUN FACT

NCAA

Football—and other sports too—are an important part of college life. NCAA stands for the National Collegiate Athletic Association. The NCAA was founded in 1906 primarily to govern football, but now this organization runs all sports played by its member schools.

Find the Flag

Can you find the seven times the word FLAG is hidden in this game of flag football?

George "Papa Bear" Halas

George Halas played for the company football team at a starch plant in Decatur, Illinois, in the 1910s. Under his leadership, his company team became the Decatur Staleys of the National Football League. He moved the team to Chicago and renamed it the Bears in 1922. Halas ran pretty much the entire Bears organization: he played, he coached, he recruited, and he even sold tickets! In recognition of Papa Bear's contributions to his team and to the NFL, the Bears uniforms show Halas's initials, GSH, on the sleeve.

TV Makes Football Popular

In the 1950s, most people could afford TV sets at home. Television networks figured out that people loved to watch football. Televised football made the game even more popular and provided a good deal of money for team owners. The Super Bowl, first played in 1967, became the most important sporting event in America. Fans enjoyed watching their favorite college players competing for many years as professionals.

Nowadays, you'll see both college and pro football on TV—college on Saturday, pro on Sunday. Many college teams and almost all pro teams sell out their stadiums every week. High schools and youth leagues stage games each week as well, giving more people a chance to play the game.

Rules of the Game

At first glance, football's rules are very complicated. The official rulebook is more than 200 pages long. In any game that you watch, you'll probably see at least one play when the announcers aren't quite sure why a referee made a call. But you don't need to know every little detail to know how to play. Just know the basics, and you'll figure out the complex stuff over the years.

The Simple Rules

A football game consists of four quarters, two in each half. In high school, the quarters are twelve minutes long. In college and in the NFL, the quarters are fifteen minutes long. Whichever team has more points at the end of the four quarters wins.

If the game is tied, the teams usually play overtime. The rules for overtime are different for different levels of play. In the NFL, the teams play a fifth quarter, and whoever scores first wins. At other levels, the teams take turns trying to score from the same spot on the field.

A football field has a 100-yard playing field and two ten-yard end zones. The field is divided in half, and each team gets an end zone. The offense scores points by getting the ball into the other team's end zone, and the defense protects its end zone by keeping the other team as far away from it as possible.

Scoring

In all levels of football there are four ways for the offense to score.

1. Touchdown—six points. Run the ball into the end zone or catch the ball in the end zone.
2. Extra point—one point. After a touchdown, the offense gets one free play. If they kick the ball through the goalposts, they get one more point.
3. Two-point conversion—two points. Instead of kicking an extra point after a touchdown, the offense can try to get the ball into the end zone. If they succeed on that play, they get two more points.
4. Field goal—three points. Kick the ball through the goalposts.

Offensive Rules

A play starts when the center hikes, or snaps, the ball between his legs to the quarterback. Until the snap, the offensive players must not move. Usually the quarterback does one of two things after the snap:

- He gives the ball to a running back, who runs with the ball behind his blockers.
- He drops back to try to pass the ball to a receiver while the blockers protect him.

On a running play, all of the offensive players are supposed to block. This means that they push the defensive players out of the way so that the running back has room to run. On a passing play, the receivers run down the field, trying to get open so they can catch a pass,

WORDS to KNOW

OFFENSE AND DEFENSE: The team of eleven players that controls the ball is the offense. They try to run or pass the ball down the field toward the end zone. The team of eleven players without the ball is the defense. They try to tackle the offensive player with the ball, and they try to knock down or intercept passes.

WHAT IS A PLAY?: In soccer or basketball, once the game starts, it keeps going for a long time. In football, once someone is tackled, the game stops for everyone to line up and start again. A play is the action that happens after the ball is hiked and before someone is tackled. Plays can usually be described as passing plays or running plays.

SACK: When the defense tackles the quarterback before he has a chance to pass the ball, that's called a sack. Bruce Smith, who played most of his career for the Buffalo Bills, sacked the quarterback 200 times and holds the all-time NFL record.

WORDS to KNOW

HOLDING: Neither offensive nor defensive players are ever allowed to hold a player who doesn't have the ball. This means no jersey grabbing, hugging, or tackling. Holding usually results in a ten-yard penalty. (Of course, the defense is supposed to do these things to the person who's carrying the ball!)

PASS INTERFERENCE: When a pass is in the air, the defense can't make contact with the receivers. If they do, the penalty is called pass interference, and it usually costs fifteen yards—sometimes even more in the NFL.

Football GREAT

Glenn Scobey "Pop" Warner

Pop Warner was a standout football player at Cornell University who went on to coach college football for forty-five years, starting in 1895. He is the one who had the idea for players to wear numbers, and he also introduced the huddle and many other common football techniques. He supported a youth football league in Philadelphia in the 1930s. The league eventually became the Pop Warner Conference.

while the linemen stay near the quarterback to block the defenders trying to sack him. If one of the receivers catches the ball, then he can keep running. However, if the ball hits the ground before anyone catches it, that's called an incomplete pass and the offense has to try again from the same spot.

Whether they run or pass, the offense has to keep moving if they want to keep the ball. They have four plays, called downs, to advance ten yards. If they make the ten yards, they are awarded a first down, and they keep the ball. If they don't get those ten yards, then the defense gets the ball.

Fourth down is the offense's last chance to finish gaining their ten yards to keep the ball. Often, the offense realizes that they're probably not going to get a first down. So they can choose to punt, or to kick the ball down the field. The other team then gets the ball, but way farther back than if the offense hadn't punted.

Defensive Rules

The defense, like the offense, is allowed to put eleven players on the field. Unlike the offense, the defense can move around before the snap. On running plays, defensive players are allowed to collide with blockers to knock them out of the way while they try to tackle the ballcarrier. On passing plays, though, there are stricter rules about contact. No one is allowed to interfere with a receiver trying to catch the ball.

The defense's job is to keep the offense from getting a first down. They can do even better, though, by forcing a turnover. If a runner drops the ball, the defense can pick it up and keep the ball. If the defense catches a pass, that's called an interception, and the defense gets to keep the ball.

You Can Play Too

Most college and professional football players are well over six feet tall and weigh more than 200 pounds.

You'd never be able to tackle them, even if you and all of your friends tried together. But that doesn't mean you can't play football. Kids' football leagues make sure that everyone, no matter how big or small, can play. How do they do that?

One way of making a game competitive is to be sure that all the players are about the same size. The country's oldest and best-known youth football organization, Pop Warner, takes this approach. Kids as young as five years old can join a team, and there are divisions for kids up to sixteen years old.

Pop Warner teams play tackle football in helmets and pads, and the rules are adjusted a bit for the ages of the players. (For example, the five- to seven-year olds can play on an eighty-yard field.) Games are just like high-school games, with ten- to twelve-minute quarters. However, unlike at higher levels of football, in Pop Warner every player must participate in every game. In fact, the rules provide a penalty for teams that don't play all their players.

Pop Warner teams compete in local leagues, usually playing about six to eight games each fall. But the teams start with practice—lots of practice. Each year, players spend a week or so conditioning then learning the fundamentals of blocking and tackling before they even put on pads. Then, more practices in pads are required. By the time the team is ready for the first game, everyone on the team knows what to do. Football is a complicated game, so the practice time pays off when it's time to compete.

All of the Pop Warner teams nationally are broken into associations of a few local teams each. The winner of an association can advance to playoffs, with each round consisting of the winners of a larger and larger area. With enough wins, a team can even advance to the national tournament in Orlando, Florida. There, the best teams nationwide from each age group play off to crown a national championship. In fact, the midget (eleven- to fifteen-year-old) division final game is usually shown on national television.

FUN FACT

Is Football Safe?

The short answer is yes. In studies conducted by many organizations, including the Mayo Clinic, it has been shown that kids in tackle football leagues suffer 10–15 percent fewer injuries, including serious injuries, each year than kids in soccer leagues. Injuries do happen, but football is no more dangerous than any other sport you might want to play.

USA Football

Though the NFL doesn't directly sponsor any leagues, it created an organization called USA Football that supports all youth football leagues. You can go to its site (*www.usafootball.com*) for information on a league close to you, training sessions, health and safety in football, or even how to become a football official.

Of course, there are other youth football organizations besides Pop Warner. In some areas, each city sponsors teams. There are also police leagues, independent leagues, Boys and Girls Club leagues, county leagues, even leagues of elementary or middle school teams. Most of these leagues operate similarly to Pop Warner—they match players of similar age and size, provide equipment and coaching, and play a weekly schedule.

Skills For Every Type of Player

One of the great things about football is that most anyone can find a position that they're good at, especially on a kids' team. The three most important features of a football player are strength, speed, and football smarts. At your age, all of these skills are best developed by playing a lot. The more games you play, the stronger, faster, and smarter you'll become, just through experience. Older players—starting in high school—put themselves through complex weightlifting or speed training programs. That's important for older players, but until you get to high school, just play as much as you can and you'll find that your body grows into its skills.

When you read the chapters on offense and defense, you'll see the specific skills that are necessary to play each position. If you are one of the fastest folks in your class, then you should try playing receiver or cornerback. If you're one of the biggest or strongest, then you could be a linebacker, a lineman, or a running back. And if you can throw the ball and make quick decisions, you might be an excellent quarterback.

Some people grow stronger, faster, or smarter than others. We can't all have the body of Brian Urlacher or the intelligence of Peyton Manning. You have to remember that you are not yet fully grown. You might think you're too slow to be a receiver. But as your legs get longer and your muscles bigger, your speed will improve. If you know exactly where to throw the ball but your arm

The **EVERYTHING KIDS'** Football Book

is too weak to get the ball there, don't give up the thought of being a quarterback. Keep practicing for a few years, and you could find that all of a sudden your throws are right on target. On that same note, remember that the folks you play against are also not fully grown. If you're the biggest player on your team, you might think that you should stick to playing offensive line or running back. What happens, though, if next year your teammates are all your size or bigger? There's no reason you shouldn't try playing every position, learning the necessary skills, and having fun.

Football is a Team Game

All this talk about what position you want to play and how you can get better is definitely important, but a football team usually has at least twenty-two players on it. The number one goal is for the team to win. That might mean you have to play your second-favorite position. Your coaches know what's best, and you have to trust them to balance the goals of playing everyone and winning as well.

You might even have to wait your turn to play. If you aren't in the game and your team scores a touchdown, cheer with them just as if you had been playing. Everyone will see what a good sport you are and what a great, positive attitude you have, even when you don't get to do exactly what you want. Maybe later in the game you'll get your chance. Don't you hope that when you score, your teammates celebrate with you?

Backyard Football

Organized youth football leagues only play one game per week, but you want to play more

Woofball

Use a light color of marker to highlight all the letters that are **not** W, F, or B. Read the highlighted letters to find the silly answer to the riddle!

What do you get when you cross a dog with a football player?

F	A	B	B	F	W
B	W	F	G	W	F
O	F	F	B	F	W
W	B	L	W	B	D
F	E	F	W	N	W
B	F	W	F	F	B
F	B	R	W	F	E
C	W	F	W	F	F
W	E	B	F	I	B
F	B	W	V	F	W
W	E	B	W	B	R

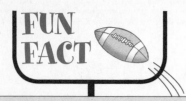

FUN FACT

Safety First

It's not smart to play full-contact football without pads, especially if some of the players are smaller than others. Blocking and tackling are certainly an important part of the official game of football, but you can design games that focus on other football skills by making up different ways to tackle and block.

TRY THIS

Buy Some Flags!

One way to give yourself the chance to play football more often is to have some flags available in your house. The best kind of flag football belt fastens with Velcro or with a loose clip so that the whole belt comes off when it's yanked. Put a big set of flags in a bag, and bring the bag with you anytime your friends get together.

football than that, right? While a school or community league is the only way to get involved in tackle football with pads and helmets, there's no reason you can't play a scaled-down version of the game on a playground or in your backyard.

Tackling

One noncontact substitute for tackle football is flag football. In flag football, everyone wears a loose belt with ribbons, called flags, on it. Instead of tackling the player with the ball, you pull the flags off of the ballcarrier's belt. Flag football can be played by people of all ages and with all sorts of different rules. In the leagues sponsored by the NFL, teams of five players play on a fifty-yard field. In another version of flag football that is played on college campuses, teams of seven players play on an eighty-yard field. Of course, you can play anywhere—just put some cones or books on the ground to show where the end zones are.

Probably the most common way to simulate tackle football is to play touch football. When someone touches the ballcarrier with both hands, the play ends. Since no equipment at all is required (other than a ball, of course), touch football is perhaps the most widely played version of the sport.

Blocking

You can avoid tackling people in your backyard by playing touch or flag football, but how do you block? If everyone's about the same size, and especially if most of you have learned proper blocking form, you might just block normally. But a more common method used in flag football is to block like you play defense in basketball: shuffle your feet, and establish a position so that no one can get by you. Then, if someone runs you over, he's committed a foul (like charging in basketball).

You can eliminate the blocking parts of the game altogether. Unless you have a huge number of players, make the rules so the offense usually passes, and make it difficult to rush the quarterback. Here are some ideas.

- Use a rush count. This means that anyone who wants to rush the quarterback has to stay at the line of scrimmage and count out loud: "one-Mississippi, two-Mississippi . . . The rusher can cross the line after "five-Mississippi."
- Make every two completions worth a first down. You don't have a chain gang on the playground, anyway. Backward passes, or passes thrown behind the line of scrimmage, don't count. This way, the offense is still allowed to run, but they're usually going to pass in order to keep getting first downs.
- Don't let the quarterback run with the ball unless the defense crosses the line of scrimmage. Just like you can let the defense blitz once every four downs, you can let the quarterback run once every four downs.
- Only let defenders who lined up ten yards behind the line of scrimmage rush the quarterback. This rule makes the game a bit more like real football, but it still gives the quarterback enough time to throw passes.

WORDS to KNOW

LINE OF SCRIMMAGE: The line of scrimmage is where the referee places the ball at the beginning of a play. Neither the offense nor the defense is allowed to cross the line before the ball is snapped and the action begins. Forward passes may only be thrown from behind the line of scrimmage.

BLITZ!: When you're playing with a rush count, you can allow the defense to blitz once every four downs. On the playground, a blitz just means the defense can rush without counting.

Backyard Football for Just a Few Players

Flag and touch football work best with teams of five to seven players. But what if you don't have enough for teams that big? Or what if you have an odd number of players so that the teams don't divide evenly?

Dealing with an odd number of players is simple. Make the person who can throw best the steady or all-time quarterback. This player plays quarterback for both teams. If several people want to play quarterback, then rotate who gets to be steady QB every four touchdowns or so.

Chapter 1: Playing the Game

CHAIN GANG: In an official football game, a ten-yard chain is carried along the sideline to determine the yardage necessary to make a first down. The people who hold the chain, put it in the right spot after each play, and carry it out for a measurement are called the chain gang.

With teams of three or four, you can use a small field. Put a cone or something at midfield for the first-down marker. Make the rule that you have four plays to get past the cone for a first down, then you have four more plays to score a touchdown.

Kicking Without Goalposts

Unless you are a true football fanatic, you probably don't have goalposts in your backyard. You'll need to change the rule about extra points. Give the team that scores a touchdown one free play. They have the choice of trying for one or two points:

- If they spot the ball at the three-yard line, they get one point for getting into the end zone on their free play.
- If they instead spot the ball at the ten-yard line, they get two points for getting into the end zone.

Field goals are more difficult. You can just make the rule that field goals don't count in your game, so everyone has to try for touchdowns. Or you can put a cone ten or twenty yards from the end zone, and a team who gets past this cone can automatically choose to take three points for kicking a field goal. Another option is to award a field goal for a team that can kick the ball so it lands in a small circle in the end zone. Be creative. You can find all kinds of ways to make field goals part of the game, even if you can't actually kick it through the uprights.

Competitive Football Skill Games

Sometimes you just can't get a real game going when you don't have a lot of people to play. You can still have some football fun, though. Try playing some games similar to drills at a football practice. Here are some ideas:

- **Man-to-man coverage:** The quarterback says "hike," and a receiver runs out for a pass. One defender tries to intercept or knock down the pass. The receiver gets one

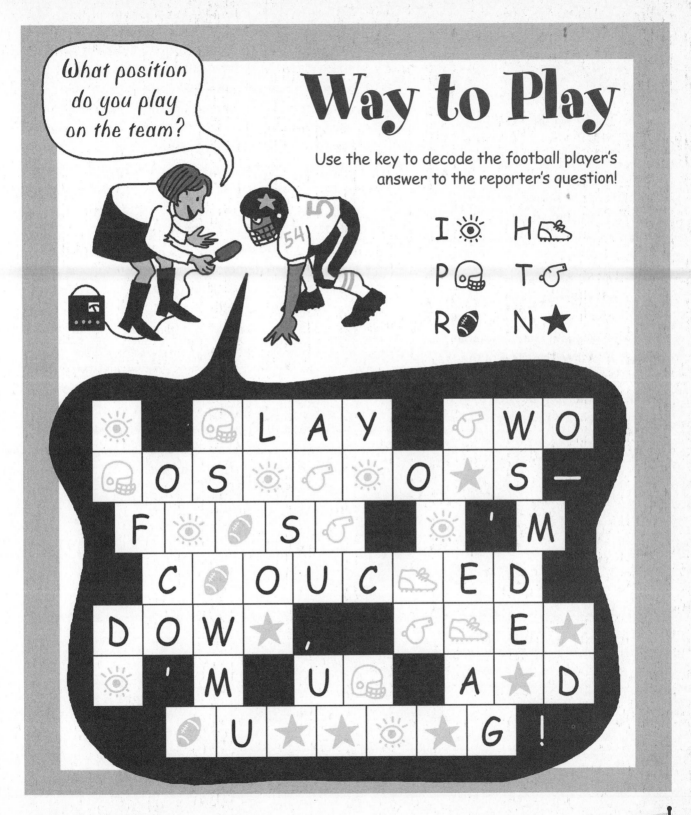

The NFL Quarterback Challenge

Every year, the NFL's quarterbacks compete in a series of challenges designed to show who has the best passing skills. Keep an eye out for the challenge to be shown on TV; it's on at a different time every year. If you want some fun passing games or if you just want to become a better quarterback, watch the challenge and then try a few of the drills you see. Some are fun and easy to do in your backyard—except that you probably can't throw the ball fifty yards like the NFL quarterbacks can.

point for a complete pass, and the defender gets two points for an incompletion. Make a time limit of, say, three seconds for the quarterback to release the ball.

- **Target accuracy game:** Set up a bunch of targets—long cones, chairs, or tree trunks work fine. Assign each target a point value, with closer or bigger targets worth less. Put a bunch of footballs in front of a quarterback. Someone says "Go!" and times thirty seconds. The quarterback tries to earn as many points as possible by hitting the targets with the ball. Everyone else races to return the thrown balls to the quarterback. Then it's someone else's turn. See who can get the most points in thirty seconds.

- **Pass pattern game:** This one takes a few more people. Use three receivers and two defenders. The receivers go out for a pass, but they all have to start and to stay on only one side of the field. The quarterback has to throw the ball within three seconds. The receiver is down right after catching the ball. Give the offense one point for each yard they get on a completion; give the defense twenty points for an incompletion. You can adjust the scoring depending on the size of the field and the skill of the defenders. The offense should be able to win since they outnumber the defense, but a clever and quick defense can do well.

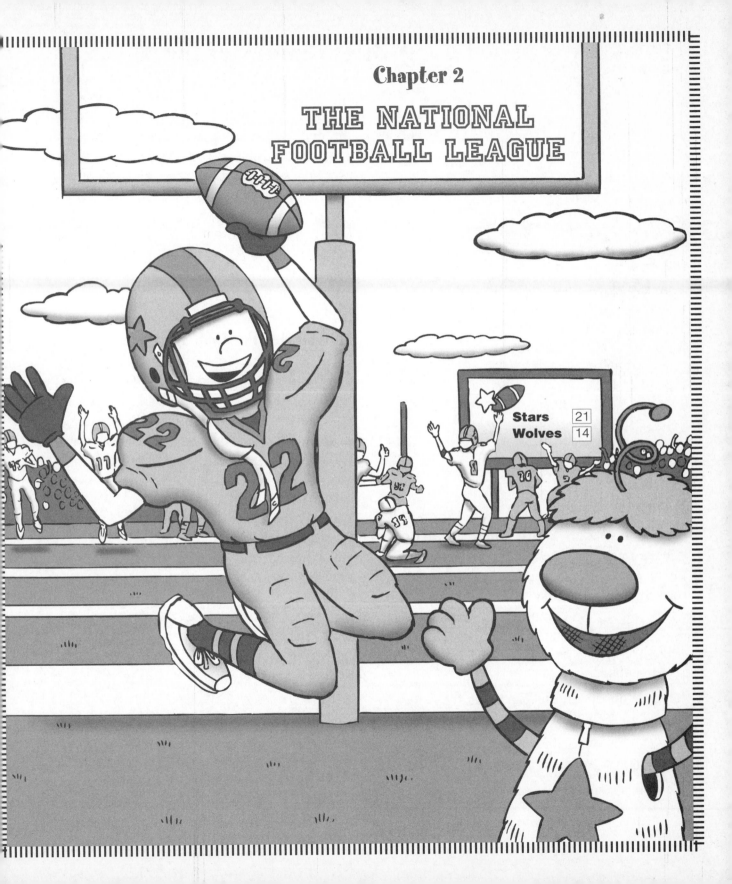

A Brief History of the NFL

In the early days of American football, the best-known teams were college teams, mainly from the Northeast. But in the working-class manufacturing towns of the Midwest, amateur teams from city athletic clubs played hard-fought games against one another. In order to gain a competitive edge against other cities, clubs began paying money to recruit the best players.

In 1920, fourteen teams made up the American Professional Football Association, which was renamed the National Football League two years later. "National" was a funny name for the league, since the teams were only from a small part of the nation.

The All-America Football Conference

The NFL had a very hard time surviving in the 1930s and 1940s. In the Great Depression of the 1930s, many families didn't have enough money to feed themselves, let alone to pay to watch football games. The economy improved in the early 1940s, but the best football players had to fight in World War II. When the war ended in 1945,

TABLE 2-1

The American Professional Football Association

These were the fourteen teams that started the association that became the NFL. Only one of the teams was located outside the Midwest, and only two of these franchises are still playing today:

Akron Pros	Dayton Triangles
Buffalo All-Americans	Decatur Staleys (still playing as the Chicago Bears)
Canton Bulldogs	Detroit Heralds
Chicago Cardinals (still playing as the Arizona Cardinals)	Hammond Pros
Chicago Tigers	Muncie Flyers
Cleveland Tigers	Rochester Jeffersons
Columbus Panhandles	Rock Island Independents

The EVERYTHING KIDS' Football Book

huge numbers of athletic young men were returning from military service. People had extra money to spend. The NFL's owners were looking forward to big profits.

But in 1946, a competing league began to play: the All-American Football Conference. The AAFC put teams in many NFL cities, like Chicago and New York.

The NFL refused even to acknowledge the existence of this new league. In fact, when a major sports magazine included the AAFC in a football preview issue, the NFL banned that magazine's writers from its games! But there was no denying that the AAFC was popular. More people were going to AAFC games than to NFL games.

Paul Brown and his scouting staff for the Cleveland Browns did better than any other team in recruiting the most talented young players, and so they ended up dominating the AAFC during its four years of play. The fact that the Browns were so much better than any other team led to the league's downfall, which played its last game in 1949. Three teams from the AAFC—the 49ers, the Browns, and the Baltimore Colts—joined the NFL the next year, while the other teams ceased to exist. It was another decade before the NFL faced another serious challenge from a new football league.

The NFL Championship Game

Before 1933, the NFL held no playoffs, just a regular season. The champion was the team with the best record. In 1932, though, Chicago and Portsmouth were tied for first place. The teams played a one-game playoff to determine the champion. This game was so popular that starting in 1933 the NFL divided its teams into two conferences and planned an NFL championship game between the conference winners. An additional divisional playoff game was played if two teams tied for the top spot in a division. Winning the NFL championship was, for forty-five years, the greatest honor in professional football. The Super Bowl didn't exist until the 1966 season.

The First Professional Football Player

In 1892, the Allegheny Athletic Association paid Pudge Heffelfinger $500 to play in a game against the Pittsburgh Athletic Club. That amount of money is equivalent to about $10,000 today. That sounds like a lot, but even a rookie in today's NFL makes nearly $20,000 per game, and most players make a lot more.

The Legendary Paul Brown

Paul Brown was perhaps the best football coach ever. He won state championships at Massillon High School in Ohio. Later, he won national championships with the Ohio State Buckeyes. So when he was appointed as the first head coach of the AAFC's Cleveland Browns, he was already famous—so famous that the NFL's Cleveland Rams left to become the Los Angeles Rams before they would have to compete with the Browns.

FUN FACT

Arena Football—in 1932!

The NFL scheduled a one-game playoff between Chicago and Portsmouth to be played at Wrigley Field in Chicago in December. A giant snowstorm hit the Chicago area the week before the game, and then it got cold—really, really cold. So the NFL decided to play the game inside! The teams played on a special eighty-yard field indoors at Chicago Stadium, the same building where the Chicago Blackhawks hockey team and, later, the Chicago Bulls basketball team, played.

The NFL kept exactly this format all the way through 1966. In 1967, it divided each conference into two divisions. The division winners played off to determine a conference champion, and the conference champions played in the NFL championship game.

Another New League and Expansion

Professional football reached new heights of popularity in the 1960s. Television networks showed games on Sunday afternoons, exposing more of the country to the game. Pro football finally started to become as important and as well known as college football.

The surge in pro football's popularity made room for other teams. But the successful NFL owners were hesitant to add franchises. So a number of businesspeople, led by Lamar Hunt, formed a new league: the American Football League. The AFL had three major advantages over the leagues that had tried to challenge the NFL before. First, the AFL owners had made their money in other businesses, so if their team lost money at first, they would have some left over. Second, the league signed a network television contract before it even started playing. Television meant that the AFL would get national attention even if its games weren't well attended. And third, the AFL owners held a player draft and shared some of their income with each other. This meant that no one team was likely to dominate the league from year to year and that every team would have a chance to win each game, so people would be interested in watching the games.

Expansion

The NFL, of course, did not like competition. It finally agreed to add a few more teams: the Vikings, Cowboys, Falcons, and Saints all joined the NFL in the 1960s. But the AFL expanded too, adding the Miami Dolphins and

Lost Player

What's going on? To find out, think of a word that best fits each of the clues. Write the word on the numbered line, then transfer each letter into the grid. Work back and forth between the grid and the clues until you get the silly answer to the riddle!

Why did the football coach shake the vending machine?

1	2		3	4	5	6	7	8		9	10	11
12	13	14	15	16	17	18		19	20	21	22	!

Where you wear a glove

‾9‾ ‾20‾ ‾5‾ ‾8‾

Opposite of loud

‾12‾ ‾13‾ ‾10‾ ‾2‾ ‾6‾

Opposite of dry

‾3‾ ‾7‾ ‾16‾

Piece of equipment that stops a car

‾19‾ ‾15‾ ‾14‾ ‾22‾ ‾17‾

What happens when a car doesn't stop

‾21‾ ‾18‾ ‾4‾ ‾11‾ ‾1‾

Football GREAT

The Undefeated 1972 Dolphins

In 1972, the Miami Dolphins became the first team to win every game in a season. The team capped its 14-0 regular season with three postseason victories, including a 14-7 victory over the Redskins in Super Bowl VII. Members of the 1972 Dolphins still celebrate together each season after the last undefeated team loses a game.

the Cincinnati Bengals. Teams were offering more and more money to players, trying to get them to switch leagues.

Chiefs owner Lamar Hunt and Cowboys owner Tex Schramm led a campaign to merge the two leagues into an expanded NFL. They agreed to play a championship game between the AFL and NFL winners starting after the 1966 season, which was the beginning of the Super Bowl. In 1970, the two leagues joined. There were ten AFL teams and sixteen NFL teams, so the Baltimore Colts, Cleveland Browns, and Pittsburgh Steelers agreed to join AFL teams in the new American Football Conference, the AFC. The remaining thirteen teams formed the National Football Conference.

A few years after Hunt and Schramm's agreement, most people thought the NFL to be a far better league than the AFL. In the first two AFL-NFL championship games, the NFL's Green Bay Packers soundly defeated their AFL opponents. NFL fans and owners wondered whether agreeing to play against such bad teams had been a smart move. But in the third AFL-NFL championship game (in what is now known as Super Bowl III), the AFL's New York Jets beat the NFL's Baltimore Colts by nine points, even though the Colts had been favored to win by more than two touchdowns. The AFL's Kansas City Chiefs blew out the NFL's Minnesota Vikings in Super Bowl IV after the 1969 season. When it came time in 1970 for the leagues to actually merge, they did so as equals.

Bigger and Bigger and Bigger

The NFL was not done expanding. In 1976, the Seattle Seahawks and the

Tampa Bay Buccaneers joined the league, the Carolina Panthers and Jacksonville Jaguars joined in 1995, and the Houston Texans were created in 2002. But expansion was about more than just adding new teams in new cities. After the merger, the NFL set about to grow in every possible way.

For a long time before 1960, NFL teams played twelve games in their regular season. That number increased to fourteen games per season in 1961. In 1978, the sixteen-game season that is still played today began.

Starting with the merger in 1970, the playoffs were expanded to ten teams: six division winners and four wild card teams. In 1990, two more wild card teams allowed twelve teams in the playoffs. More playoff games meant more television money and more big events. The NFL season, which used to be completely over in December, stretched into late January.

More Teams, More Games, More Playoffs

NFL expansion created new and more dedicated fans. Every city wanted a team, but the NFL couldn't just add an unlimited number of teams. Cities started convincing owners to move their teams. The Oakland Raiders moved to Los Angeles in 1982, though they moved back to Oakland in 1995. Before the 1984 season, the Baltimore Colts moved to Indianapolis in the middle of the night. The St. Louis Cardinals became the Arizona Cardinals in 1988, but St. Louis got a new team in 1995 when the Rams relocated there. The Houston Oilers moved to Tennessee to become the Titans in 1997. The Cleveland Browns moved to Baltimore in 1995 to become the Ravens, and a new Browns team was created in 1999.

Why did all these teams move? In most cases, the new city offered the owner a brand new stadium and lots of money. These new stadiums were more comfortable than the old ones and included more luxury boxes. The new cities had plenty of folks willing to pay enormous

WORDS to KNOW

THE MERGER: Officially the AFL merged with the NFL in 1970, even though they had played championship games since the 1966 season. You will often hear broadcasters refer to events "since the merger." Though team and individual statistics before 1970 are official and do count in the record books, the year of the merger represents when the NFL started to resemble the league you watch today.

WILD CARD: Before 1970, the only teams in the playoffs were the division winners. In the 1970 season, the two teams in each conference with the best records that were not division winners were invited to the playoffs. These teams played each other in the wild card game. The winner of that game advanced to play a division winner.

amounts of money for season tickets, and plenty of rich people or companies ready to pony up for the luxury boxes. Owners found that by even threatening to move to a new city, their original city would often build a new stadium just to keep the team from moving. In 2007, twenty-one of the NFL's thirty-two teams played in a stadium that had been built since 1980. Four of the remaining teams are building new stadiums right now.

Television, Satellite TV, and the Internet

One final area of growth for the NFL came from television and other media coverage. The year 1970 marked the debut of Monday Night Football, which was among the most watched television programs every week. For a long time, you could watch only three games per weekend: two games on Sunday and one game on Monday night.

In the mid-1990s, the NFL made it possible for fans to watch all of its games. If they pay lots of money, fans

Find the Football

Find the one time that FOOTBALL is spelled correctly. Look up and down, side-to-side, and backwards!

```
      T A B O O L O F
    F O O T T O B A O L O O
    B F O O F O F O O T T B A L L
    T A O L F L O O F O O B L A L F
  F O O T B F O O O T B A L A L O O F
F O O T O L T A O B B O L F L F L O A B
F O O B T L L A B T O O F B O F T O
B A A O F O O T T O F B A L F O
    F L O T B A F O L O F O T O
      L F O O T A O A O L L O
      T O O L B A T O
```

with a special kind of satellite TV can choose to watch any game being played. In the mid-2000s, a satellite radio service made it possible to listen to all of the games on radio. While you can't yet watch live games over the Internet, you can pay to listen to all of the games online. The NFL Network began broadcasting in 2003, showing footage from training camps, the draft, practices, and, starting in 2006, some live games.

The Biggest Event in America: The Super Bowl

The AFL-NFL championship game was named the "Super Bowl" by Chiefs owner Lamar Hunt. Super indeed. After more than forty years, Super Bowl Sunday is an unofficial national holiday. The game has become much more than just a league championship. Many Americans—at least one-third of the population—watch the game on television, and many people throw parties and watch with their friends and families. Super Bowl XLII in 2008 was the most watched Super Bowl ever; an average of 97.5 million people were tuned into the game at any given moment. The only sporting event in the world that is more significant is soccer's World Cup.

Super Bowls are numbered starting with Super Bowl I after the 1966 season. This is because the regular season lasts from September through December, but the championship game isn't played until the next year. The New York Giants won the Super Bowl in 2008, but they were the champions of the season that was played in fall 2007.

I. Packers 35, Chiefs 10. This was the first AFL-NFL championship game, but it wasn't yet called the Super Bowl.
II. Packers 33, Raiders 14. Packers coach Vince Lombardi won his last world championship.
III. Jets 16, (Baltimore) Colts 7. Joe Namath's Jets

FUN FACTS

Most Super Bowl Victories
The Cowboys, 49ers, and Steelers have all won five Super Bowls, more than any other team. The Cowboys have made it to eight Super Bowls, which is the most by any team.

Roman Numerals
The NFL uses Roman numerals to number the Super Bowls. You may have learned about these in school. Roman numerals use letters to represent numbers: I means 1, V means 5, X means 10, and L means 50. It gets a bit more complicated—IV means 4, while VI means 6, because you subtract if the smaller number comes first. The following list goes in order, so you can figure out for yourself how to count to forty-two in Roman numerals.

MVP
Bart Starr of the Green Bay Packers was the MVP for the first two Super Bowls, and Joe Namath earned the honor in Super Bowl III. Starr and Namath also share the same alma mater, the University of Alabama.

Brush Up

This coach is giving one of his players a compliment—or is he?
To find out what the coach is saying, you must write all the letters
from the scattered pieces into their proper spaces in the grid.
Hint: Try matching the pattern of the black boxes!

showed everyone that the AFL was just as good as the NFL.

IV.   Chiefs 23, Vikings 7.

V.   (Baltimore) Colts 16, Cowboys 13. Chuck Howley of the Cowboys was voted the game's most valuable player, even though his team lost.

VI.   Cowboys 24, Dolphins 3.

VII.   Dolphins 14, Redskins 7. The 1972 Dolphins became the first team in NFL history to complete an undefeated season.

VIII.   Dolphins 24, Vikings 7. The Dolphins were the first team to appear in the Super Bowl three years in a row.

IX.   Steelers 16, Vikings 6. The Vikings lost their second of four Super Bowls.

X.   Steelers 21, Cowboys 17. The Steelers came from behind with two touchdowns in the fourth quarter, then intercepted a pass on the last play of the game.

XI.   Raiders 32, Vikings 14. Raiders head coach and hall of famer John Madden won his only Super Bowl.

XII.   Cowboys 27, Broncos 10.

XIII.   Steelers 35, Cowboys 31. The Steelers won again in the matchup of the greatest teams of the 1970s.

XIV   Steelers 31, (Los Angeles) Rams 19. The Steelers won their fourth Super Bowl in four tries.

XV.   Raiders 27, Eagles 10.

XVI.   49ers 26, Bengals 21. San Francisco quarterback Joe Montana led his team to a 20-0 halftime lead. The San Francisco defense forced five turnovers.

XVII.   Redskins 27, Dolphins 17. Washington quarterback Joe Theismann won his only Super Bowl.

XVIII.   (Los Angeles) Raiders 38, Redskins 9. This would be the last victory for the AFC for fourteen years.

XIX.   49ers 38, Dolphins 16. In his only Super Bowl

Football GREAT

Joe Namath

Jets quarterback Joe Namath guaranteed his team would win Super Bowl III, even though the Colts were heavily favored. Namath proved the media and the analysts wrong and earned the MVP award in the game. He was one of professional football's first superstars, appearing in movies and TV shows when he wasn't playing football.

John Madden

You may know John Madden from his NFL video game or his work as a television commentator, but that's not why he's in the Hall of Fame. Madden was drafted by the Philadelphia Eagles in 1958, but his career was cut short by injury. He found real success as a coach. As the head coach of the Oakland Raiders, he racked up the highest regular season winning percentage of any coach with 100 career victories.

FUN FACT

Eureka!

Gold was discovered in California in 1848, and large numbers of gold diggers flocked to the West Coast starting in 1849. The new arrivals were nicknamed 49ers. Nearly 100 years later, the All-America Football League created a franchise in San Francisco, and the team took on the 49ers name. Sourdough Sam, the 49ers mascot, is a cheerful football-loving gold digger.

appearance, Miami quarterback Dan Marino lost to Joe Montana's 49ers.

XX. Bears 46, Patriots 10. Coach Mike Ditka led his overwhelming favorite Bears to a convincing victory.

XXI. Giants 39, Broncos 20. Giants coach Bill Parcells won his first of three Super Bowl appearances.

XXII. Redskins 42, Broncos 10. Skins quarterback Doug Williams not only became the first black quarterback in the Super Bowl, but he was the game's MVP.

XXIII. 49ers 20, Bengals 16. Joe Montana threw the winning TD to John Taylor with 34 seconds remaining, but 49ers receiver Jerry Rice was the MVP.

XXIV. 49ers 55, Broncos 10. Ho-hum, Joe Montana won his fourth Super Bowl and his third MVP award.

XXV. Giants 20, Bills 19. Scott Norwood's 47-yard field goal attempt went wide right as time expired.

XXVI. Redskins 37, Bills 24.

XXVII. Cowboys 52, Bills 17. Dallas quarterback Troy Aikman won his first of three Super Bowls.

XXVIII. Cowboys 30, Bills 13. The Bills tied the Vikings and the Broncos with four Super Bowl appearances and four losses.

XXIX. 49ers 49, Chargers 26. This time the 49ers were led by quarterback Steve Young, who threw six touchdowns.

XXX. Cowboys 27, Steelers 17.

XXXI. Packers 35, Patriots 21. QB Brett Favre led a resurgence of the Packers franchise, which had not seen such good times since the days of Vince Lombardi.

XXXII. Broncos 34, Packers 24. Though the Broncos had lost four previous Super Bowls, they won this time behind a tremendous rushing attack.

XXXIII. Broncos 34, Falcons 19. Quarterback John Elway

Perfect Play

Give yourself six points if you can match this touchdown to its perfect shadow!

won his second straight Super Bowl and the MVP trophy as well.

XXXIV. Rams 23, Titans 16. The Titans had one last play from the ten-yard line, but Mike Jones tackled receiver Kevin Dyson at the one-yard line to seal the game.

XXXV. Ravens 34, Giants 7. The Ravens defense dominated this game, allowing only a special teams touchdown.

XXXVI. Patriots 20, Rams 17. Kicker Adam Vinatieri nailed a 48-yard field goal to end the game. First-year starting quarterback Tom Brady was MVP.

XXXVII. Buccaneers 48, Raiders 21. The Tampa defense intercepted quarterback Rich Gannon five times, returning three for touchdowns.

XXXVIII. Patriots 32, Panthers 29. Once again Adam Vinatieri won the game with a last-second field goal, and once again quarterback Tom Brady was the MVP.

XXXIX. Patriots 24, Eagles 21. Vinatieri, Brady, and coach Bill Belichick won another close game.

XL. Steelers 21, Seahawks 10. Receiver Hines Ward and running back Jerome Bettis were the offensive heroes of the Steelers, who had just barely made the playoffs.

XLI. Colts 29, Bears 17. Peyton Manning, who had been a top-rated quarterback for seven years without a championship, showed he could come through in a big game.

XLII. Giants 17, Patriots 14. MVP Eli Manning led two fourth quarter touchdown drives to defeat New England, who had not lost a game all year until the Super Bowl.

Who Are These Teams, Anyway?

Nowadays, the NFL's thirty-two teams are divided into two conferences: the American Football Conference (AFC) and the National Football Conference (NFC). These conferences can be traced back in league history to the AFL-NFL merger in 1970. The AFC consists mainly of old AFL teams, and the NFC consists mainly of original NFL teams. Each conference is broken into four divisions with four teams in each division.

Each team plays sixteen regular season games. With thirty-two teams, it's not possible for a team to play every other team in a season. Instead, each team plays a schedule that depends on what division they're in. Your team will play two games against each team in its own division, six other games within their conference, and four games against the other conference. For example, each year the Falcons play two games against the Panthers, two against the Saints, and two against the Buccaneers. They also play six games against other NFC teams (different teams every year), and they play four games a year against different AFC teams.

Table 3-1

AFC East	AFC West	AFC North	AFC South
Miami Dolphins	Oakland Raiders	Cincinnati Bengals	Indianapolis Colts
New York Jets	Denver Broncos	Pittsburgh Steelers	Jacksonville Jaguars
New England Patriots	San Diego Chargers	Cleveland Browns	Tennessee Titans
Buffalo Bills	Kansas City Chiefs	Baltimore Ravens	Houston Texans
NFC East	**NFC West**	**NFC North**	**NFC South**
Philadelphia Eagles	St. Louis Rams	Green Bay Packers	New Orleans Saints
Dallas Cowboys	Seattle Seahawks	Minnesota Vikings	Carolina Panthers
Washington Redskins	Arizona Cardinals	Chicago Bears	Atlanta Falcons
New York Giants	San Francisco 49ers	Detroit Lions	Tampa Bay Buccaneers

The EVERYTHING KIDS' Football Book

Playoffs

After the sixteen-game season, the best teams get to play in the playoffs. In playoff games, whichever team wins gets to play again the next week, and the losing team is done for the season. The last playoff game is the Super Bowl, and the winning team is the NFL champion.

A total of twelve of the thirty-two teams, six in each conference, make the playoffs. Figuring out which teams get into the playoffs isn't easy. Here are the guidelines:

- The winning team in each division makes the playoffs.
- In each conference, the two teams with the best records that aren't division winners also make the playoffs. These two teams are called wild card teams.

Once the playoff teams are determined, the play-off schedule is set. The first weekend after the regular season is wild card weekend. The wild card teams play against four of the eight division winning teams. The two teams in each conference with the best records earn a bye, meaning they don't have to play a game during wild card weekend. Instead, they get an extra week off.

After wild card weekend comes the divisional play-offs, in which the teams with byes play the winners from wild card weekend. In the next weekend, the winners play the conference championship games, after which only two teams are left—the AFC champion and the NFC champion. These are the teams that go to the Super Bowl.

The Bosses

Have you ever heard television reporters talk about a team's power structure? They don't mean the offensive line. Though the players play the games, there's a whole group of people on every team who determine which players play and how they play. A team's power structure consists of, among others, the coach, the general manager, and the owner.

FUN FACTS

Tiebreakers

The hard part of figuring out who's in the playoffs comes when teams finish the season with the same record. The NFL tiebreaker rules are quite complicated. Games within a division and games between teams in the same conference are most important when determining who wins a tiebreaker. You can read the details at *www.nfl.com*.

Preseason Games

Starting in August, each team plays four preseason games. These do not count in the standings, so the best players don't usually play much. Instead, you'll see some of the backup players competing for jobs.

Belichick's Rough Start

Bill Belichick's first head coaching job was with the Cleveland Browns from 1991 to 1995. There, his teams compiled a losing record and only went to the playoffs once. Sure, he's probably a better coach now than he was then. But the Patriots organization probably works better with Belichick's style than did the Browns.

The Coach

The head coach is responsible for preparing his team for each game. In the game itself, the head coach makes strategic decisions, like whether to punt or to try for a first down. NFL football is so complicated that a head coach can't run everything alone. The head coach hires a large number of assistants, who take charge of smaller aspects of the team. For example, the linebacker coach teaches the linebackers how to play their positions, and the defensive coordinator coaches the entire defense and is in charge of each week's defensive game plan.

At first glance, coaching seems pretty easy. It's the players who have to run and tackle, and the coaches just watch, right? But coaching is exhausting in a different way. Coaches watch game film all the time. They look at their next opponent, trying to find weaknesses. They look at their own games, evaluate players, and figure out how to make their own guys more successful. Players show up at practice, work hard, and go home when they're done. Coaches prepare for practice just like a teacher prepares for class. Once practice is over, the coach goes right back to preparing.

A winning NFL team requires great players as well as great coaching. It's not always fair to judge a coach as good or bad based on his record in one or two seasons. Yet it's reasonable to say that the best coaches are those who have led their teams to the playoffs many times over the years. For example, one of the absolute best NFL coaches today is Bill Belichick of the New England Patriots. He was named head coach in 2000. From then through the 2007 season, the Patriots' season record has been 107-

37, they've been to the playoffs in seven of nine years, and they've won three Super Bowls.

Jeff Fisher of the Tennessee Titans has been his team's head coach longer than anyone else in the NFL. Over fourteen years, his teams have won 54 percent of their games and have gone to one Super Bowl. The only recent coach who's been in charge longer than Fisher was Bill Cowher of the Pittsburgh Steelers. He won 62 percent of his games over fifteen years. He retired after the 2006 season, a year after winning the Super Bowl.

The General Manager (GM)

The coaches figure out what to do with their players. But a coach can't just ask any old player to join his team. A team must first sign that player to a contract and agree to pay him a salary. It is the general manager's job to find and sign players to fill out the team.

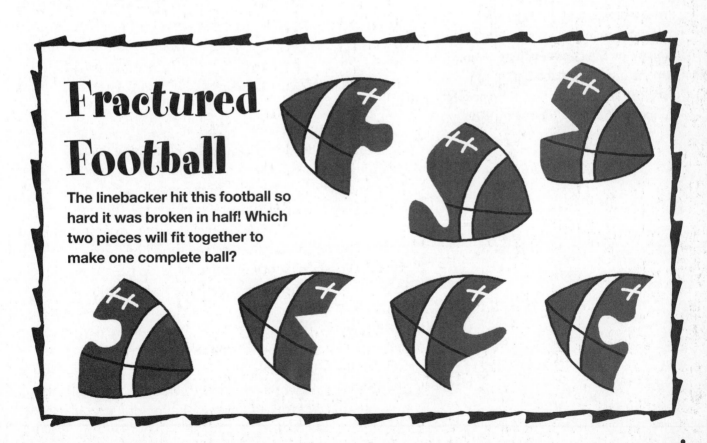

Fractured Football

The linebacker hit this football so hard it was broken in half! Which two pieces will fit together to make one complete ball?

FUN FACTS

Shopping for Players?

Some coaches are willing to put in the extra work to gain the extra control of being able to sign and coach players. As legendary coach Bill Parcells once said, "If they want you to cook the dinner, at least they ought to let you shop for some of the groceries."

How Long Do Coaches Last?

The Redskins have had five different head coaches in the eight years since Dan Snyder bought the team. On the other hand, the Pittsburgh Steelers are on only their third coach since the AFL-NFL merger in 1970.

This is a more complicated job than you might think. Each team is only allowed to spend a certain amount of money each year. This salary cap means that if a star player wants a lot of money, the general manager either needs to let that player go to another team, get rid of another player, or pay other team members less so that he can afford to sign the star. If a general manager wants a player who is already signed to a contract by another team, the GM has to negotiate a trade. Perhaps the most visible part of a GM's job comes on draft day, when each team's GM takes turns picking former college players to be part of their teams. Figuring out which players to draft requires intensive scouting and lots of research. The NFL draft is shown on national television so that fans everywhere can see the decisions each team makes right away.

On just a very few teams, the head coach also serves as the general manager. Doing both jobs requires a lot of work for one person. Most teams want different people in those two roles, partly to give each person more time to concentrate on the job, and partly to give two different points of view to the construction of the team.

The Owners

Head coaches and GMs worked for many years at lower-level football jobs. These folks proved their worth before being hired to such an important position. No matter how good coaches or GMs become, though, they're not going to work their way up to become owners. The owner of a franchise is simply the person who bought the team. Football knowledge isn't required to buy an NFL team, but having a lot of money is. For example, Dan Snyder bought the Washington Redskins in 1999 for $750 million. In 2006, it was estimated that he could sell the franchise again for almost twice that price. *Forbes* magazine's research suggests that the average NFL team is worth about $900 million dollars, with many teams costing well over $1 billion dollars.

The EVERYTHING KIDS' Football Book

An ideal owner buys the team, hires a strong GM and an outstanding coach, and lets them make all the football decisions. If the GM or the coach isn't performing well, it is the owner alone who has the power to fire them. That's often a difficult decision for an owner, especially an owner who knows little about the ins and outs of an NFL team. If the team didn't make the playoffs this year, is it because the GM did a poor job of obtaining players? Were the players good enough but poorly coached? Or was it a really good team that just hit a few bad breaks and will be very good next year? It's usually quite hard to tell the difference. Since it's easier to fire the coach than to fire all the players, the coach is very often the one who pays the price for a bad season.

Be a Part of the Action

Most NFL stadiums have room for 70,000 people. Being one of those 70,000, all cheering at the top of their lungs for the home team to win, is an experience that you will treasure for a long time. If you get a chance to go, be sure to look around you, see everything that is happening, and really savor the trip.

Getting Tickets

Ticket prices for NFL games are very, very high. It costs an average of $70 for just one ticket to one game, and that's for an average ticket in an average-priced stadium. A premium ticket to a New England Patriots game costs more than $500!

To get tickets, go to www.nfl.com and click "tickets." Then click on the team whose game you want to go to. You'll read instructions about how to purchase the tickets you want. Most NFL tickets are sold as season tickets. To get a season ticket, you pay the team for ten tickets, and you get to sit in the same seat for all eight regular season home games and for the two preseason home games.

Be Prepared!

NFL games go on in 100-degree heat as well as in heavy snow. Check the forecast ahead of time, and bring anything you think you might need. It's better to have a pair of gloves in your pack that you never use than to spend three hours at the game with frozen hands, wishing you had brought the gloves!

Dressing Up

You don't have to wear a Halloween-style costume to an NFL game, but it is sometimes fun. Look at the fans around the stadium. Many will be wearing team jerseys, of course. But a few will have elaborate outfits with special hats or painted faces. Dressing up adds to the fun!

Very often, it's just impossible to buy tickets for a team's games. The tickets were sold years in advance. For example, the Arizona Cardinals not only sell all their season tickets every year, they also have thousands of people on a waiting list, hoping just to get the chance to buy a ticket someday. So how can you go to a game? The other way to go is to find a friend or relative who has season tickets. Sometimes, season ticket holders can't go to all the games, so they'll give away (or sell at face value) their seats to one or two games. Some teams have online ticket exchanges where season ticket holders can resell game tickets. You won't be able to schedule your game very far in advance, but you might be able to grab a couple of tickets a few days before the game.

Be careful—don't buy an NFL ticket from someone you don't know and trust. Most teams do not allow tickets to be sold for more than face value. Furthermore, tickets that look real might be fake. Tickets have bar codes on them that tell the computer who bought the ticket. If your ticket doesn't check out with the computer, you won't be allowed in.

At the Game

Before you go, ask someone or look online for advice about getting to the stadium. With 70,000 people trying to cram into one building, crowds can get huge and lines can get long. Find out where to park and if there's a better way to get to the stadium than by car. If you can park across town and take a bus or a train, do it—you'll save lots of money and time.

Also, read up on stadium rules about what you can bring with you. It makes sense to bring a backpack containing things like bottles of water, sunscreen, a poncho, a hat, sunglasses, or any other personal items you might want. You can carry your souvenirs home in the backpack, too. But before you go, be sure your backpack and everything in it is allowed in the stadium.

The game will definitely be exciting, causing you and all the fans to cheer, yell, scream, and jump out of your seats. That's exactly what's supposed to happen—this isn't the opera, after all. Be sure to be considerate of others while you're cheering, though. You—and the other fans—don't need to use foul language, throw things, or be obnoxious to fans of the visiting team. Cheer as loud as you can for your team, but don't be rude and ruin someone else's experience.

During the game, watch for parts of the game you can't see on TV. For example, look at the receivers running their routes, and you'll notice parts of football that the narrow television screen can't show you. Before the game and during halftime, walk around the stadium. Most stadiums have murals, statues, or wall hangings honoring the team's history. Talk to some fans in the concession line and find out where they're from, what they know about the team, and how long they've been fans. You're at an NFL game, one of the greatest possible American cultural experiences. Make the most of it.

If You Can't Go

You can watch virtually any NFL game on television if you can't go to the game. Watching on TV is a less intense experience, but it is a lot more convenient (and a lot cheaper too). Near a city, the home team's games will almost always be shown on local network channels. If you want to watch an out-of-town team, you may have to watch on cable or satellite, but there will be a way to watch.

Most NFL games are played on Sunday afternoons. The local CBS station will pick one or two AFC games to show, and the local FOX station will pick one or two NFC games to show. On Sunday night, one special game will be shown on NBC to the entire country, announced by Al Michaels and John Madden.

WORDS to KNOW

TAILGATING: A tailgate party is a picnic in the stadium parking lot before a game. This can be as simple as eating some sandwiches out of a cooler while sitting on the back of your car. Elaborate tailgaters bring lawn chairs, big grills, and four-course meals. Part of the fun is being with all the other tailgating fans of your team. Bring extra food to share, and you'll meet some interesting folks!

FUN FACT

Monday Night Football
In the 1960s and 1970s, no more than two games were shown on TV each Sunday. In 1970, ABC started showing one game every Monday night, using their best announcers and lots of cameras and graphics to produce a big show. Monday Night Football lasted until 2005 on ABC, and every week it was one of the top ten most-watched TV shows. Now, MNF is on ESPN with the top-rate announcing team of Mike Tirico, Tony Kornheiser, and Ron Jaworski.

Football Fill In

Get ready to pass, punt, and run! If you're a rookie player, you can choose from the answer words scattered around the puzzle on the next page. Pro ball players should be able to complete the puzzle without looking!

ACROSS

2. A six-point score earned when the ball crosses the goal line

6. Player who receives the snap during a field goal attempt

9. Fake grass sometimes used in football stadiums

11. Area created by the offensive line to protect the quarterback

13. Offensive players who catch passes

14. A person or animal that represents a team

15. To throw the ball

17. A football field has 100 of these

18. Person who makes sure the teams follow the rules

21. Three points earned when ball is kicked through the goalpost

24. Arena where football games are played

25. People who cheer for a team

26. Offensive player who throws passes

DOWN

1. Person on the sideline who guides the team through plays

3. A group of players who gather together to discuss the next play

4. What the referee blows to stop a play

5. Offensive player who snaps the ball

7. Players who control the ball and try to score

8. What the fans eat in the stands

10. A group of football players who work together

12. One way to stop a player from running

16. What a player wears to protect his head

19. Game played where the school's graduates come to watch

20. A defensive player who tries to keep receivers from catching passes

21. What a referee throws to indicate a foul

22. Players who keep the other team from scoring

23. When more than four defensive players rush the quarterback

COACH

WHISTLE

CENTER

RECEIVERS

BLITZ

HOTDOGS

QUARTERBACK

HOLDER

PASS

TEAM

YARDS

HOMECOMING

TACKLE

ASTROTURF

REFEREE

TOUCHDOWN

POCKET

FANS

HUDDLE

SAFETY

DEFENSE

OFFENSE

FLAG

HELMET

MASCOT

FIELD GOAL

STADIUM

FUN FACT

The Heidi Game

At 7:00 p.m. on November 17, 1968, the Jets took a five-point lead on the Raiders with sixty-five seconds to go. Though a football game usually takes only about three hours to play, this one was taking longer. NBC television had planned to air the movie *Heidi* at 7:00, so they stopped showing the football game and showed the movie. Fans, especially in New York, were furious. So many people called NBC to complain that NBC issued an apology and changed their rules to show all football games to the end.

Sunday Rituals

The best part of watching your team on TV is that you don't have to make a big trip to still feel like you're at the game. Fans love to watch with a group of friends. You can all have lunch together before the game, or put out a bunch of snacks to eat during the game. After the game, you don't have to wade through crowds to get home, so you can relax and leave when you want. The best part is, you get to do it all again for the next week's game!

The Commentators

At the stadium, an announcer will give the crowd game information, such as who carried the ball, how many yards he gained, and who made the tackle. That's it.

On TV, though, two or three people talk all through the game. One, called the play-by-play announcer, states the basic game information. The others, called color commentators or analysts, just talk about football throughout the game. Good color analysts can teach you about the game, show you the little details that made a play work or not work, and tell you a bit about the players.

The Sunday Night Football Crew

The best-known television announcing team today works the Sunday night games: Al Michaels and John Madden. Michaels is known as the best play-by-play announcer for any sport. In fact, he started his career as primarily a baseball announcer. Michaels became famous in 1980 when he called the United States hockey team's Olympic upset of the Soviet Union with "Do you believe in miracles? Yes!" He has worked prime-time NFL football since 1986.

Madden is a Super Bowl–winning coach who spent his career with the Oakland Raiders in the 1970s. He was hired in 1979 as a color commentator. Back then, football announcers didn't get excited about much. Madden's quirky style made him popular with his fans. Madden has a fear of flying, so he travels around the country in a custom-made bus called the Maddencruiser to get to each game.

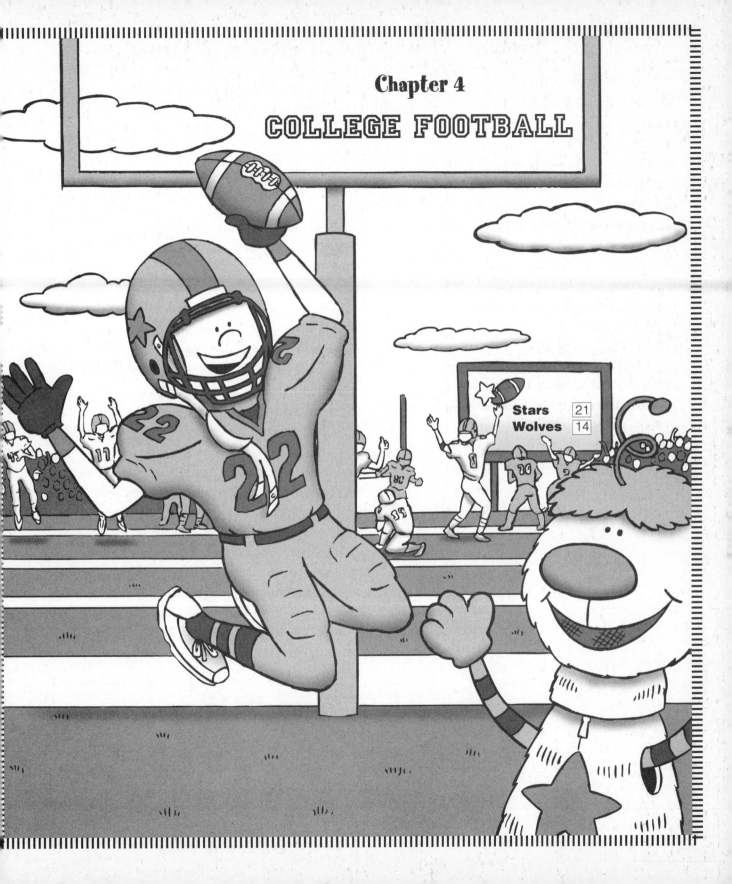

Emmitt Smith

Running back Emmitt Smith is best known for his thirteen years with the Dallas Cowboys, during which he helped lead the team to three Super Bowl victories. Because Emmitt was so successful in the pros, many fans forget his outstanding career at the University of Florida, which earned him a place in the College Football Hall of Fame. After Emmitt began playing in the NFL, he continued to take classes at Florida in the offseason. In 1996, six years after he began his NFL career, Emmitt graduated with a degree in public recreation.

What Is the NCAA?

The National Collegiate Athletic Association (NCAA) is the governing body for virtually all college football. Member schools join one of three divisions:

- Division III schools are usually small and do not formally offer athletic scholarships. In Division III, athletics are viewed as merely extracurricular activities, not as a way for the school to make money.
- Division II schools offer athletic scholarships, though they have a limited number to offer. These programs generally do not have the enormous money or fan support necessary to participate in Division I, but they nevertheless offer competitive teams.
- Division I is the most competitive level of NCAA football. Teams have large stadiums, and many fans come to watch every game. They offer large numbers of athletic scholarships. The schools make lots and lots of money from selling tickets, merchandise, and television rights.

Division I has two subdivisions:

- The Championship Subdivision used to be called Division I-AA. These are the smaller schools, which attract fewer than 15,000 fans on average to their games. At the end of the year, sixteen teams enter a playoff to determine a champion.
- The Bowl Subdivision used to be called Division I-A. These are the football powers who contend for a national championship. Virtually all of the teams you see on TV are from this subdivision. While the Bowl Subdivision has no playoffs, most of the teams are invited to a bowl game at the end of the year. The winner of the most important of these bowls is crowned the national champion.

NCAA Football Versus NFL Football

You might not notice the different kinds of players, the different schedules, the different rules of college football. Here's a quick summary.

Who Plays?

The most important difference is also the most obvious: college football players are actual college students who live on campus, go to class, and (hopefully) graduate from the school after several years. They still participate in college life in many of the same ways that physics majors do, and some of them may even be physics majors. College football players are not formally paid, though some of them are given a full scholarship. This means they don't have to pay for tuition, housing, food, or other typical living expenses.

A college football player is only allowed to play for his team for four years, while he is a student. Since it takes most students a while to develop their skills and their bodies to the necessary level, most players are starters for only one or two years. Fans get used to watching new players each year.

WORDS to KNOW

ATHLETIC SCHOLARSHIP: NFL players are paid lots of money; however, colleges are not allowed to pay their players. Instead, players are often offered athletic scholarships where all of the player's college tuition fees and living expenses are paid for him.

REDSHIRT: Often, a first-year college student isn't ready to play regularly for his team or a player might get hurt right before the season. If the team agrees to keep him out of most games, then the year becomes a redshirt year, meaning it doesn't count toward his four years of eligibility.

A Shorter Schedule

The college schedule is shorter than the NFL schedule. Play starts in late August, when most of the really good teams play weaker teams in order to start the season with some wins. Conference play begins by late September. After eleven or twelve games, the regular season schedule is complete by mid-November. Some conferences hold a championship game in early December, while the lower divisions hold national playoffs. Division I-A teams who win at least six games can be invited to play in bowl games, which usually happen in late December or early January.

Different Rules

College football is just about the same game that the NFL plays. There are a few minor differences that you'll only notice if you watch carefully. For

Super Sized

Use the picture and letter equations to spell out the silly answer to this riddle.

What kind of football player wears the biggest helmet?

THE   -C

THE B+ -P +GEST

H+ -BR !

example, college teams get the ball on the three-yard line to try for an extra point; NFL teams get the ball on the two-yard line. The hash marks, where the ball is put in play, are farther apart in college. The NFL requires a receiver to get both his feet in bounds to catch the ball fairly; college receivers only need one foot down. Both levels play for four fifteen-minute quarters, but they have different rules about when the clock stops and when it runs. As a result, college games usually take longer to play than pro games.

Perhaps the biggest difference between pro and college football is the overtime procedure. In the NFL, overtime is played just like the rest of the game, but the team that scores first wins. In college, one team gets the ball at the other team's twenty-five-yard line and tries to score. Then, the other team gets the ball at the same spot. Whoever scores more points wins. If the teams are still tied, they go again until one team comes out of overtime with more points than the other. Starting in the third overtime, teams must try to get a two-point conversion instead of kicking an extra point after a touchdown.

The Fans

NFL teams represent a city. People become fans if they grew up near the team. NCAA teams represent their school as well as their community. Most of the student body has some connection to the football team. Some students are band members or cheerleaders, and student managers help the coaches run drills. Students who aren't directly involved with the team might at least know someone on campus who is involved—maybe they're in a class with the star quarterback, or they use the fitness center at the same time as the cheerleading squad. Students usually get cheap tickets and dress in school colors ready to make noise in the crowd.

Because football is such an important part of their social life during college, people who go to colleges with football teams tend to develop a lifelong love for their team. Colleges have alumni clubs in which graduates pay money to get special seating at games, meetings with coaches, and parties at the stadium with their friends. Graduates bring their own children to games, building loyalty throughout families.

But not all fans are students and alumni. A college team draws fans from the surrounding community. Especially when there's no NFL team nearby, college football becomes the biggest event on Saturday and throughout the year. For example, most of the state of Nebraska is a long day's drive from Denver, where the closest NFL team plays. But they're not concerned. To them, it is the University of Nebraska Cornhuskers

Football GREAT

Red Grange
The Galloping Ghost first became nationally famous while he played for the University of Illinois. In a 1924 game at Michigan, he scored five touchdowns, four of which came in the first quarter. Red joined the Chicago Bears after graduation, where he earned the then-unimaginable salary of $100,000 for the season.

FUN FACT

games on Saturdays that they care most about. Los Angeles, California, hasn't had a football team since the Rams and Raiders left in the 1990s. So the two biggest college teams, the UCLA Bruins and the USC Trojans, are the true hometown favorites.

How College Football Is Organized: Conferences

More than 100 teams make up the Football Bowl Subdivision of NCAA Division I. Teams play only eleven or twelve games each year, so there's no way that a team can play every other team. A conference consists of eight to twelve teams from one region of the country and usually includes schools of similar size and stature. Each team plays most of the other teams in its conference every year.

Teams join conferences for many reasons. Most important is for money: conferences have rules to ensure that every team makes some money each year. For example, if a team plays in a bowl game, some of the money they make is distributed among all the teams in the conference. This way, a team makes money even in years when it isn't doing well. Another reason for being part of a conference is for the schedule. Since about eight of every year's games are conference games, the school only has to look for three or so other games to schedule. Of those eight or so conference games, usually about four are guaranteed to be home games. Without a conference, it might be difficult to find teams to play, especially teams that are willing to play as a visiting team.

NCAA Division I-A Conferences

The six best-known and most competitive conferences are called the BCS conferences.

- **The Southeastern Conference (SEC):** As the name suggests, these schools are all in the southeastern part of the country, from the Atlantic Ocean to Louisiana. The

SEC is divided into an Eastern and Western Division. The division winners play a championship game at the end of the season. The Tennessee Volunteers and the Louisiana State Tigers won their divisions in 2007, and Louisiana State won the championship.

WORDS to KNOW

INDEPENDENTS: An independent team is not part of a conference. Only four Division I-A teams are independent: Notre Dame, Army, Navy, and Western Kentucky.

- **The Big Ten:** You might think that a conference called the Big Ten would include ten teams, but it actually contains eleven schools. Why? The Big Ten had only ten teams from 1950 until 1990, when it added Penn State University. All of the conference's teams are in the midwest, stretching from Pennsylvania to Iowa and Minnesota. The 2007 champion was the Ohio State Buckeyes, who edged out the Illinois Fighting Illini and the Michigan Wolverines for the title. The Big Ten does not play a championship game.

- **The Pacific 10:** Nicknamed the Pac 10, this conference includes ten teams from the four western states of California, Oregon, Washington, and Arizona. The University of Southern California Trojans have dominated the Pac 10 recently, finishing at the top of the standings each year since 2002. The California Golden Bears shared the title in 2006, but Southern Cal won the league by itself in 2007.

- **The Atlantic Coast Conference (ACC):** For many years, the ACC was known for basketball. Historically great basketball programs from North Carolina, Duke, Wake Forest, North Carolina State, and the rest of the conference took the spotlight away from football. In the 1990s and 2000s the league added several football powerhouses, including Miami and Florida State. Now ACC football demands national attention. All of the league's twelve teams are from states bordering the Atlantic Ocean. Each team plays eight conference games, and the winners of each of the two divisions play in the ACC championship game in December.

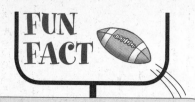

FUN FACT

The World's Biggest Mascot

At the beginning of every half, the Big 12's Colorado Buffaloes are lead onto the football field by Ralphie, a live buffalo.

- **The Big 12:** In 1994, the Big 8 conference merged with four Texas schools from the former Southwest Conference to make the Big 12. The conference members are mostly located in the Great Plains. Oklahoma defeated Missouri in the 2007 championship game.

- **The Big East:** When three of this conference's teams left to join the ACC in the mid 2000s, the Big East invited new members Louisville, Cincinnati, and South Florida. The result has been a competitive football conference, with four ranked teams in the the 2007 season. West Virginia and Connecticut shared the Big East championship in 2007.

The six conferences described above generally command the best players and the most television and fan attention. The five other Division 1-A conferences—the Sun Belt, Western Athletic, Mid-American, Mountain West, and Conference USA—are often called mid-majors:. Mid-major teams have strong programs that are competitive with each other, but they usually have a hard time when they're up against teams from the BCS conferences. In fact, a bigger program will often pay a mid-major team a lot of money to play a game at the bigger school's home field. Why? The big team gets a home game that they're likely to win. The mid-major team may not like the idea of getting crushed in a road game, but the money they make might pay for a large number of scholarships or a new fitness center. And who knows? About once or twice a year, a mid-major beats a big-time team.

Determining a National Champion

The NCAA Football Bowl Subdivision is the only college sport without a tournament to determine the official championship. Instead, throughout the year football reporters and football coaches vote on who they think are the best teams. A set of computer experts uses the season's results and mathematical formulas to rank the teams. The rankings from reporters, coaches, and computer programs are combined into a special ranking called the BCS. After the regular season, the top two teams in the BCS play in the BCS National Championship Game.

The winner of the BCS National Championship Game is recognized by the NCAA as the national champion. However, occasionally, the final reporters' poll of the year ranks a different team number one. In that case, the national championship is shared by the BCS winner and the number one team in the reporters' poll. This happened in 2003. Louisiana State University won the BCS championship, but the reporters voted Southern Cal as the best team. Both teams are considered to be 2003 national champions.

Table 4-1

National Champions

Year	Champion
1990	Colorado Buffalos and Georgia Tech Yellow Jackets
1991	Washington Huskies and Miami Hurricanes
1992	Alabama Crimson Tide
1993	Florida State Seminoles
1994	Nebraska Cornhuskers
1995	Nebraska Cornhuskers
1996	Florida Gators
1997	Michigan Wolverines and Nebraska Cornhuskers
1998	Tennessee Volunteers
1999	Florida State Seminoles
2000	Oklahoma Sooners
2001	Miami Hurricanes
2002	Ohio State Buckeyes
2003	Louisiana State Tigers and Southern California Trojans
2004	Southern California Trojans
2005	Texas Longhorns
2006	Florida Gators
2007	Louisiana State Tigers

Cold, Blue Turf?

Bowl games are usually played in warm places like Hawaii, Florida, or California. But one bowl game is played in the very cold city of Boise, Idaho. The field for this bowl game is artificial turf, not natural grass—and the turf is painted blue! Rumor has it that migrating geese sometimes crash into the blue turf because they think it's a lake!

Bowl Games

You might now be saying, "Huh? Why no NCAA football tournament? Why is the national championship so complicated?" The answer has to do with what are called bowl games.

The Way It Was

Before the 1990s, the BCS didn't exist. Rather, the winner of each conference earned a spot in a bowl game. The best known bowl was the Rose Bowl in Pasadena, California, which pitted the winner of the Big Ten against the winner of the Pac 10. The Southwest Conference winner went to the Cotton Bowl in Texas, the Big 8 winner went to the Orange Bowl in Miami, and the SEC champion went to the Sugar Bowl in New Orleans. These four bowl games were all played on New Year's Day.

The bowl games back then were extra special and extra popular. In those days, most people couldn't see more than one or two college football games per week. If you lived, say, in Ohio, you might never have seen a Pac 10 game all year. The bowl games were the fans' opportunity to see some of the great teams they had heard so much about. As for the teams, only the winner of a conference or a few selected other great teams got to play in a bowl. Bowl games meant long trips to exotic cities, with all expenses paid for the players. It also meant more people watching than ever before.

Bowl Games Today

Today, there are thirty-two bowl games played in the weeks before and the week after New Year's Day. Any team that wins six games—even if it also lost six games—is eligible to play in a bowl. More than half of the Division I-A teams play in a bowl. Of the teams in BCS conferences, virtually all play in a bowl. Now that most regular season games are on television through-

The EVERYTHING KIDS' Football Book

out the country and almost any team can make it to a bowl, bowls are not as big a deal as they used to be.

But they're still fun! Millions of fans still watch the games and the players have a good time. NCAA rules say that any team that makes it to a bowl game is allowed extra practice time to prepare. Teams make use of this time not only to get ready for the bowl, but also to give younger players experience so they'll be ready to replace the graduating seniors the next year. Most bowls may not be truly special games, but they'll keep being played as long as people keep watching.

The Best College Football Rivalries

Most schools have a single most hated rival, a team they play only once each year but whose game dominates the season. A true rivalry means that, during the first part of the season, fans of both teams actively root against their rival, no matter who they play. A team would rather go 1-10 while beating their rival than go 10-1 with a loss to their rival. Most rivalry games are played the week before Thanksgiving, though some are played Thanksgiving weekend.

Here is a look at the four best-known college football rivalries:

Alabama Versus Auburn

The Iron Bowl matches the two biggest football schools in the state of Alabama. It is said that anyone who moves into Alabama is immediately asked to declare whether they are an Auburn or an Alabama fan. The teams didn't play each other between 1907 and 1947 because the schools couldn't agree on how to get unbiased referees. The Auburn Tigers have won six more games than the Alabama Crimson Tide in the history of the rivalry.

Making Bowl Games Exciting to Watch

One way to generate some interest in all thirty-two bowl games is to have a contest with your friends and family. When the matchups are announced, print out a list of all the games. Have all the contestants pick the team they think will win each game. After all the games are over, whoever picked the most winners wins a prize!

Rivalry Story

The 1995 movie *Crimson Tide* takes place aboard the submarine the USS Alabama. In one scene, the boat's crew shouts out the University of Alabama rallying cry, "Go Bama! Roll Tide!" But when Auburn fans saw this scene in the theater, they shouted out their own team's battle cry, "War Eagle!"

FUN FACTS

The Stanford Axe

At a Cal-Stanford baseball game in 1899, Cal students stole an axe from the Stanford cheerleaders. Cal kept that axe in a bank vault for thirty-one years, until a crew of Stanford students launched an elaborate and successful plot to steal it back. Now whichever team wins the Big Game gets to keep the axe for a year. At Stanford pep rallies, cheerleaders still refer to "the Stanford Axe that California has wrongly stolen from us, that it is our responsibility to retrieve."

Rivalry Story

Legendary Ohio State coach Woody Hayes hated Michigan—not just the university, but the whole state and anything associated with it. It is said that when the Ohio State team bus was running out of gas on the way home to Ohio, Coach Hayes refused to stop at any gas station in the state of Michigan, even if he might have to walk for miles to get more gas.

California Versus Stanford

The Big Game, as it's known, pits these San Francisco Bay area schools against each other each year. Both schools are best known for their strong academic programs, and they have produced plenty of NFL players. In the days leading up to the game, the California freshmen chemistry classes all get together for a special demonstration in which the professor turns a red flask blue with just one drop of a chemical. (Red is Stanford's color; blue and gold are California's colors.) The most famous play in college football history occurred at the end of the 1982 Big Game. Stanford quarterback John Elway had just led his team on a drive to take the lead with four seconds on the clock. But on the kickoff, the Cal team made five backward passes and evaded all of the Stanford tacklers. The Stanford band, thinking the game was over, started to march onto the field. Cal's Kevin Moen ran among the band members and entered the end zone, where he knocked over an unsuspecting trombone player. Cal won the game 25-20.

Michigan Versus Ohio State

These schools have each won seven national championships, and together they have won nearly half of all Big Ten championships in conference history. As a result, the yearly Michigan-Ohio State game rarely fails to get national attention. There is nothing more important to fans of these schools than beating their rival. Former OSU coach John Cooper won more than 70 percent of his games and three conference championships. But his record against Michigan was 2-10-1, so he was fired in 2000. In 2006, the two teams were ranked first and second in the nation, and the hype surrounding the game was intense. Retired Michigan head coach Bo Schembechler passed away the day before the game, adding even more emotion to the rivalry game. In the end, the Buckeyes beat the Wolverines 42-39.

Go Team!

A very visible part of any football team are the cheerleaders! The first organized cheer was during a college football game over 100 years ago, in 1898. Believe it or not, that original cheer is still being used at the University of Minnesota today! Use the decoder to fill in the blanks, and then give this cheer a try—outside the house, of course!

A = ✳
H = ★
I = ☆
N = ✰
O = ✩
S = ✳
Y = ◎

R✳★, R✳★, R✳★!

✳K☆-U-M✳★,

★★✰-R✳★!

★★✰-R✳✩!

V✳R✳☆T✩!

V✳R✳☆T◎!

V✳R✳☆T◎,

M☆★✰✳-E-✳★✰-T✳★!

FUN FACTS

Bill the Goat

Bill is the Naval Academy mascot. He's a live goat who attends every Army-Navy game. He has been kidnapped several times in history, by cadets at both Air Force and Army, but each time Naval Intelligence tracked him down and obtained his release.

The Commander-in-Chief's Trophy

This coveted award is presented to the team with the best record in the yearly games between Army, Navy, and Air Force. Though Air Force has won the trophy the most times, Navy has won the past five trophies from 2003–2007.

Army Versus Navy

Each branch of the United States armed forces has its own academy. To attend, a student must meet very strict academic and physical requirements. Everyone at the service academies, not just the athletes, gets a full scholarship. All students take challenging courses and receive military training, and they must spend several years in the armed forces when they graduate. Student life is quite different at Army and Navy (and Air Force) than it is at other Division I schools.

It's understandable, then, that the academies aren't usually in the hunt for a national championship. Yet the Army-Navy rivalry is perhaps the most intense in the country. Cadets and Midshipmen arrive at the game in Philadelphia in full uniform. They put on displays of pushups when their team scores. The game is carried on the Armed Forces Network, meaning that everyone in the Army and the Navy, even people who are deployed overseas, can watch the game on television or listen to it over the radio. The game has always been an important television event in the United States. In fact, the first time that a replay was ever shown during a televised football game was during an Army-Navy game.

College Football Beyond Division I

Every year, thousands and thousands of good high school football players graduate and go to college. Only the very best are offered scholarships for Division I teams. Though the majority of these high school graduates will never make it to the NFL, they might not be ready to end their football careers. One option for them is to play football at a Division II or a Division III school.

Lower-division colleges don't have 100,000-seat stadiums and national television cameras at the games. At the same time, their games are usually much bigger events than high school games, with large stadiums, big crowds, and a high quality of play. Fans of lower-division football teams point out that going to their games can be a better experience than going to a big school's games because admission is cheaper, the stadium is less cramped, and there's no need to fight for a parking space.

Perhaps the most fun aspect of Division II and III football is the national championship playoff at the end of the season. The very best teams get to host as many as three playoff games at home. The national final in each division is shown on national television. The Division II championship is played at the University of North Alabama every year. Valdosta State won the title in 2007 and has won two of the last four championships.

What's in a Name?

All college teams have some kind of nickname. Frequently animals are used for both the nickname and the team mascot. Break the Letter Switch code (B=A, C=B, D=C, etc.) to learn the four most popular animal nicknames!

Some teams choose more unusual nicknames. Break the Vowel Switch code to learn some of these lesser known mascots!

FBHMFT   CVMMEPHT   UJHFST   MJPOT

PONGIANS   KONGOREES   EWLS   BLIU HUNS

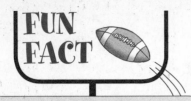

Eddie Robinson

In 1941, Grambling State University, a Division I-AA college in northern Louisiana, hired coach Eddie Robinson. Until 1997 (that's fifty-six years!) Robinson coached the Tigers to 408 victories, the most ever for a coach in Division I. More than 200 of his players entered the NFL. That would be a lot for a huge Division I-A program, let alone for a coach in a lower division.

In Division III, the championship game is called the Amos Alonzo Stagg Bowl, named after the famous coach of the University of Chicago's football team from the early 1900s. The Stagg Bowl is played each year in Salem, Virginia. In 2007, Mount Union College, winners of eight of the past eleven Division III titles, and the University of Wisconsin-Whitewater squared off for the championship for the third year in a row, and Wisconsin-Whitewater prevailed to win its first title.

There's a Team for Everyone

The pros take center stage on Sundays, and college football seems to dominate autumn Saturdays in America. But Friday nights belong to the high schools. Most high schools, public and private, sponsor a football team. Since most teenagers attend high schools within their local area, high school teams truly represent communities. You have probably met some of the players on the nearby high school team, and you might even have relatives on a team. Perhaps you'd like to play high school football one day.

Varsity, Junior Varsity, and Freshman Teams

The team that represents the school on Friday night includes the best players in the school, and it is called the varsity team. The majority of varsity players are juniors and seniors. Unless a younger player is unusually fast or way bigger than normal for his age, he's probably not ready to play varsity.

Depending on the size of the school, there might be other teams to join. The junior varsity (JV) team often includes players who are not quite good enough to play regularly on the varsity, or perhaps players who are good enough to play varsity but who are still too young or too small to make a regular contribution. The JV team might play on Monday instead of Friday or might play a Friday afternoon game as a prelude to the varsity game. If the school is big enough, it might sponsor a third team, one just for freshmen. The lower-level teams give you the best way to play the game, have fun, and develop your skills. The best way to become good enough for the varsity team is to play hard and to play well at the freshman and JV level.

The Offseason—Getting in Shape

The game of football requires enormous physical effort, and it can give your body a bit of a beating. You must be

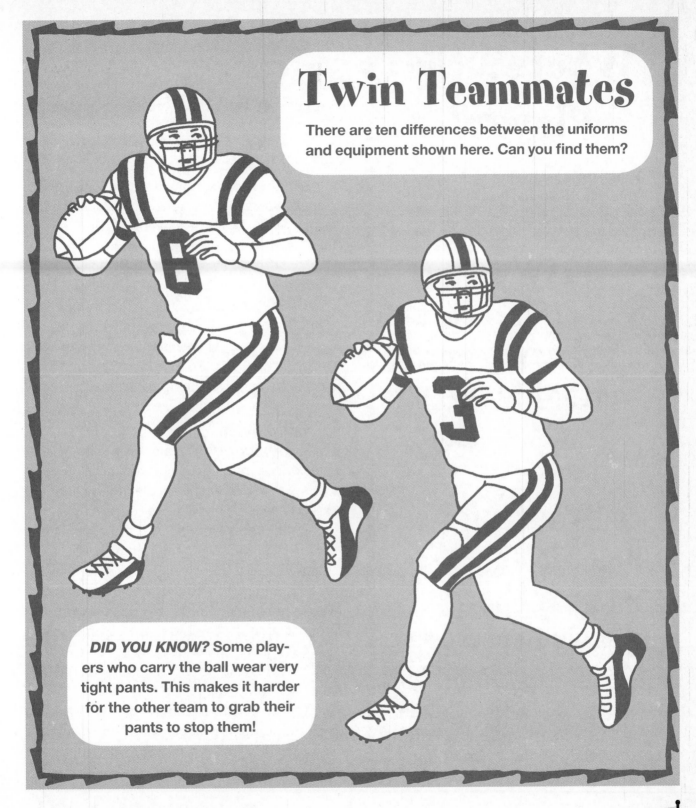

Twin Teammates

There are ten differences between the uniforms and equipment shown here. Can you find them?

DID YOU KNOW? Some players who carry the ball wear very tight pants. This makes it harder for the other team to grab their pants to stop them!

Where's the Player?

Break the Last to First code to read this silly riddle and its silly answer!

hatW si het
ifferenced
etweenb a
ootballf layerp
nda a uckd?

. . . .

ou'llY indf neo
ni a uddleh,
nda het thero
ni a uddlep!

---

in good shape to play any kind of football, and the higher the level of your game, the more speed, strength, endurance, and flexibility you must develop. A high school football player cannot spend all summer just lying on the beach and playing video games. Someone who does so will likely not make it through the first practice, let alone any games.

A high school coach will usually give the players a summer workout program that will gradually build up the players' fitness. The idea is to come into preseason practices ready to play hard. Offseason workouts include lots of running and weightlifting. The team might come in all together a couple of times per week for their workouts. Players who go on long vacations or who do special summer trips can still run, do pushups and sit-ups, and find a place to do weightlifting occasionally.

Skill Camps

The summer is the time when many colleges offer camps to help players develop their skills. These may last a couple of days or as long as a week. The college's coaching staff often runs these camps. They show the players drills, films, and conditioning exercises that will help them develop into better players. The camps can be a chance to compete against and practice with top players from other schools. By the end of the camp, everyone has a pretty good idea of what he can do well, which skills still need improvement, and who the really, really good players are.

A great way for a team to improve together over the summer is to play in a 7-on-7 league or to attend a 7-on-7 camp. Sure, it's important to develop individual skills, but it's even more crucial to play with your teammates in competitive situations. In a 7-on-7 game, quarterbacks can practice reading coverages and can learn how their receivers will react to different defenses. Defensive backs can practice not just one-on-one defense, but can be part of an entire coverage scheme. If you're playing a game, then what you're doing feels like more than just practice. A great play can actually score a touchdown, just as in a real football game, and a mistake may cost points. The team is practicing under nearly real game conditions. When the team is faced with a truly real game in the fall, they will know how to react. They will have confidence in their teammates and in themselves, hopefully leading to a few extra wins.

Right Before the Season

The team gets together for two weeks or so of preseason practice. The coaching staff usually has two goals for this time:

- Teach the team how plays are called and what to do on each play.
- Improve players' techniques so everyone becomes a better player at his position.

To accomplish these goals, many different teaching tools might be used. For example, the team might have classroom meetings with a chalkboard and notebooks to explain how some plays are supposed to work. On another day the team might watch video of a college team executing these plays successfully. Sometimes it's useful to watch video of yesterday's practice to show who ran the plays correctly or incorrectly.

On the field, a chunk of practice is devoted to skill development with the position coaches. During this time, the players run drills that help them practice a technique. For example, quarterbacks may work on hitting a target, or on reading the safeties and throwing

TRY THIS

What is 7-on-7?

In a 7-on-7 drill, the offensive and defensive lines are removed so the team can focus just on the passing game. The defense plays with three linebackers and four defensive backs; the offense gets a center, five running backs or receivers, and a quarterback.

The Tip Drill

One of the defenders' favorite drills is called the tip drill. In one version, the coach throws a pass to a running receiver, who deliberately misses the catch and tips the ball in the air. The defenders have to catch the ball for an interception. If they can't catch the ball cleanly, they're taught to try to keep the ball in the air. Defenses love interceptions, of course, and they can make an interception on every play of this drill.

away from them. Linebackers may repeatedly practice taking a read step and dropping into coverage.

Another big chunk of preseason practice time is devoted to rehearsing plays. The offense might start by running the plays on air, meaning that they just go through what they're supposed to do without any defense around. Next, a few managers or second-string players might hold pads and stand where defenders might be. Eventually, the offense knows the plays well enough to run them against a live defense.

Scouting the Opponent

Once the season starts, both the offense and the defense usually know all of the team's plays. The question then becomes which of these plays will work best against the next opponent. Figuring out which plays to use is called scouting, and it is one of the coaching staff's biggest jobs.

Well before each game, teams trade tapes. They send video of their old games to their next opponent. The weekend before a game, the coaching staff watches this tape carefully. First, they figure out who the opponent's best players are and which are the best units. They'll also try to find the other team's weak spots. Perhaps their cornerbacks look really good, but their defensive linemen seem to get pushed back on every play. Then they decide what strategy to use to beat this team. Perhaps on offense they need to use a power running game, mixed with a few deep passes if the safeties come up to stop the run. Whatever they decide, the coaching staff must have a clear plan ready before Monday's practice: that's when they start preparing the team for the game.

The Week Before a Game

Practice during the season runs a bit differently from preseason practices. Much less time is set aside to work

The **EVERYTHING KIDS'** Football Book

on skills and techniques because more time is necessary to establish and practice the week's game plan.

The Scout Team

Most football teams include a good number of players who don't get much playing time in games. These folks aren't the starters, and sometimes they aren't even the backups for the starters. But they can play an essential role in practice.

Once the coaching staff has scouted the upcoming opponent, they know how that opponent plays: what formations they use on offense, which kinds of plays they run, and what strategies they use on defense. To prepare for this opponent, the coaching staff chooses a scout team made up of nonstarters. The scout team pretends to be the upcoming opponent. Their job is to give the starters practice seeing the same kind of football team that they will see on Friday night. If enough players are available, two scout teams could be formed—one for offense, one for defense.

Early in the week, the coaches explain the game plan and practice the specific plays or defenses that will be used. First the offense and defense practice separately, making sure they know what to do. Toward the end of practice, the offense and defense will run against the scout team. The coaching staff can tell which of their ideas will work (and which won't) by noticing how the scout team does. If the scout team is stopping the offense, then the offense probably needs a new game plan.

By the end of the week, the players all know what to do. Practice might then consist of special game situations, like trying to score from the two-yard line or stopping the offense on third down and long. Maybe the team will even play a ghost game in which the starters and the scout team play a shortened version of a real game, complete with a coin toss, kickoffs, and coaches pretending to be referees.

Impersonating Star Players
If the next opponent has a really good player, the scout team might assign their best athlete to pretend to be that star. On some teams, the star player on the scout team gets to wear a special jersey with the number of the opposing player. Being chosen to impersonate the opponent's best player is a big deal for a scout team player.

WORDS to KNOW

HOMECOMING: One home game each fall is the homecoming game. That's when all students who already graduated come back to the school to see each other and show their support for their former high school. Homecoming events include more than just a football game—usually there's also a parade, a dance, and maybe even other events.

Pep Rally

If there's a big football game that night, students will be thinking about their team all day at school. Use the clues to help complete these words that are full of team spirit!

lunch wrappers and empty lunch bag

_ R A _ H

mistake in Drivers' Ed.

_ R A _ H

important to have in chorus

_ R _ A _ H

art project with dried flowers

_ R A _ H

what boring teachers do

_ R A _ H

_ R A _ H

activity in math class

_ R A _ H

after-school fundraiser

_ _ R A _ H

Thursday's practice before a Friday night game is usually a relaxed practice. The players are storing up their energy for the next day's game. They don't want to get banged up or sore without time to recover. But the players can still run through their plays, and they generally go through the motions of beating the opponent. By the end of Thursday's practice, the team will be ready for the game.

State Championships

High school teams play eight to eleven regular season games. Just like college teams are members of a conference, high school teams play many of their games against the same schools every year. In high school, this group of schools is usually called a district, though the term is different in some states. The regular season schedule usually includes one game against each of the other teams in the same district. Districts are chosen to include similar-sized schools from the same local area.

At season's end, the best team or teams in the district advance to the state playoffs. Though big and small schools might play regular season games against each other, in the playoffs, teams only play schools of about the same size. The state association sets up tournaments similar to the NCAA Division II and Division III playoffs. The winner of each playoff game advances to the next round. Eventually, the remaining teams are from different parts of the state. The championship games—one in each size category—are often held in a major college or NFL stadium because of the huge crowds that show up.

The EVERYTHING KIDS Football Book

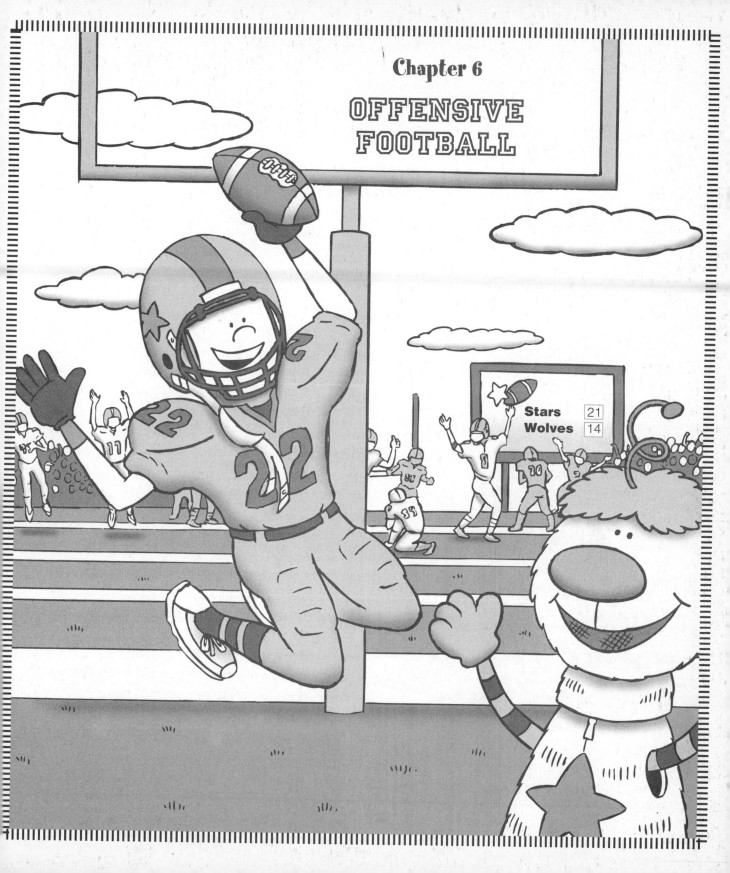

What Is Offense?

The offense is the unit on a football team that tries to carry the ball into the end zone. They can use all sorts of different plays and strategies to move the ball. At its heart, though, every play is either a running play or a passing play.

Running Plays

On running plays, the quarterback usually hands the ball to a running back. Sometimes the quarterback will keep the ball and run it himself. Either way, on running plays the offensive line tries to push the defensive team back in order to give the runner holes to run through. Running plays will usually gain a few yards. It's unlikely that a team will lose yards running the ball, but it's also unlikely that they'll make big gains. Running is especially important for a team that is trying to hold on to a lead because the clock will almost always keep counting down after a running play.

Passing Plays

On passing plays, the quarterback holds the ball and tries to throw it to one of his receivers. The offensive line doesn't push down the field; rather, it drops back and tries to keep the defensive team away from the quarterback. Passing plays are riskier than running plays—passes can be intercepted, and the offense doesn't gain any yards if a pass isn't caught. But passes are also the way to make big gains.

A good offense is balanced and includes both passing and running plays. Sure, some teams use one type of play more than the other, depending on their players' strengths. But every team must be able to both pass and run.

The precise design of passing and running plays has changed a lot over the past

The **EVERYTHING KIDS'** Football Book

century. Today, teams use all sorts of offensive schemes. A later section of this chapter explains some of the possible strategies that an offense can use. All successful offenses use the same basic types of players: a clever quarterback, a strong offensive line, and powerful or fast receivers and running backs. The first part of this chapter will explain the jobs of each type of player.

Joe Montana as . . . the Quarterback

The quarterback is the boss on the field. At the start of pretty much every play, the quarterback gets the ball, and he starts the action. Different offensive schemes may require the quarterback to do different things with the ball. For example, an option-based offense might have the quarterback carry the ball (or at least pretend to carry the ball) on every play. Most NFL offenses have the quarterback drop back five to seven steps on every play, each time either handing the ball to a running back or passing from the pocket.

Adjusting the Play

During a football game, the coach usually tells the quarterback what kind of play to run. But once the teams have lined up, the quarterback has to decide whether that play is likely to work. For example, pretend that the coach calls a running play to the right side. The quarterback should notice how the defense lines up. If the defense has a lot of players waiting on the right, where the running back is supposed to go, then the quarterback should make the decision to change the play.

One way to change a play is to use code words. Right before the snap, you'll see the quarterback shouting signals to his team. Often, those signals don't mean anything. But everyone on the team knows a few special words for plays. When the quarterback uses those code words, then everyone knows to forget the play the coach

WORDS to KNOW

POCKET: When the quarterback has dropped back to pass, his offensive line forms a pocket around him. They push the pass rushers toward the sideline and down the field, keeping the area around the quarterback clear of defenders until the quarterback can throw a pass.

Football GREAT

Joe Montana

Joe Cool, as he became known, started his career with the San Francisco 49ers in 1979. In only his third year, he led the 49ers to their best NFL season ever: a 13-3 record and a playoff berth. Joe was named the most valuable player in three of his four Super Bowl victories. Throughout his career, Joe was known for his grace under pressure. Twenty-six times he led the 49ers to come-from-behind wins. That's where the nickname Joe Cool came from. Even when his team trailed, they believed Joe could lead them back.

The Silly Answer Is
"The One in the Sugar Bowl!"

What's the silly question? To find out, use the directions to cross words out of the grid.
Read the remaining words from left to right and top to bottom!

..........................Cross out...........................

...sports that use nets   ...places to keep clothes
...two-letter words without I   ...insects that don't fly

IF	TENNIS	TWO	ANTS
ON	FLIES	ARE	BASKETBALL
EARWIGS	CLOSET	AN	FLEAS
IN	VOLLYBALL	THE	DRESSER
SPIDERS	KITCHEN	HAMPER	WHICH
AT	ONE	ROACHES	UP
IS	OR	THE	PING-PONG
BADMINTON	FOOTBALL	OF	PLAYER

The EVERYTHING KIDS' Football Book

called and instead to run a new play. The code words the quarterback uses are called audibles.

Sometimes the quarterback has options to avoid a stacked defense even after the play starts. The simplest example is that the quarterback might choose to keep the ball and run the other way if a running back is about to run into a blitzing linebacker. A more complicated example is that if he sees a blitz coming, the quarterback can throw to the "hot" receiver.

Two Dominant Quarterbacks

Peyton Manning joined the Colts in 1998 after starting for four years at the University of Tennessee. His first year was rough, and the Colts only won three games. Since then, the Colts have made the playoffs eight times under Peyton's offensive leadership and won Super Bowl XLI in 2007. Peyton runs the offense himself. Before each snap, the coach suggests two plays, and Peyton chooses from those or calls one of his own. He is a master at game strategy, reacting to anything the defense tries to do. Watch him at the line of scrimmage. Peyton is known for flapping his arms like a chicken, squawking out real and fake signals in order to tell his teammates what play to run.

How does he always know what his offense should do? Peyton is one of the best prepared football players in the NFL. He watches tape for hours, picking out defensive formations and defensive players he can take advantage of. He practices with his team but also privately with his receivers. Thanks to an excellent coaching staff and Peyton's attention to detail, the whole Colts offense can adjust their game plan moment by moment in a game.

Tom Brady was the starting quarterback at the University of Michigan for two years. He led the Wolverines to a shared Big Ten championship in 1998 and victories in the Citrus Bowl (1998) and the Orange Bowl (1999). Despite his success in college, Tom was the 199th player drafted in 2000—yet he has had tremendous success in

WORDS to KNOW

HOT ROUTES: A blitz is when lots of unexpected defenders rush toward the quarterback. The quarterback has to get rid of the ball quickly! On many passing plays, one receiver runs a very short route, called a hot route, and gets ready to catch the ball right away. If the quarterback sees a blitz, he knows he can throw right away to the hot receiver to avoid being sacked.

FUN FACT

Brady-Manning Rivalry
Tom Brady's first NFL start was a victory against Peyton Manning and the Colts in 2001. It was the beginning of an intense rivalry. Peyton would not find a way to beat Tom's Patriots until 2005. The two have faced off against each other ten times. So far, Tom holds the edge with seven wins to Peyton's three.

the NFL with the New England Patriots. He won three Super Bowls (and two Super Bowl MVP trophies) and led his team to eight straight winning seasons with seven playoff appearances.

Tom is best known for his playoff successes. Like his idol Joe Montana, Tom has repeatedly authored game-winning drives in crucial games. He has the most consecutive wins of any quarterback in the postseason with ten. He is just as good or better under the intense pressure of a playoff game as he is in the first game of the season.

Anthony Muñoz Anchors . . . the Offensive Line

A team's offensive linemen are the men who move mountains. They have one job: to block the defense. On running plays, they open up lanes for running backs to run through. On passing plays, they protect the quarterback by forming a pocket. It takes a special kind of unselfish person to be an offensive lineman. Fans rarely hear about the linemen, except when they are called for a penalty. Linemen don't usually score touchdowns, don't make tackles, and don't gain yards. Yet the line is the most important unit on the offense. A good offensive line can make a bad running back look great. By giving him time to throw, a good offensive line can make any quarterback who can throw look awesome.

The offensive line consists of the center, who snaps the ball; the two guards, who line up just right and left of the center; and the two offensive tackles, who line up just right and left of the guards.

Running Plays

The first job of the offensive line on a running play is to create a surge. The offensive linemen have an advantage over the defense because they know when the ball will be snapped. When the ball is snapped, the linemen move powerfully in the direction of the play, trying to take two steps before they contact a defender. This process is called firing off the line.

Zone Blocking

Before the snap, all the linemen have to know their responsibilities. They have to know which direction to fire off the line, and they have to know if there's a specific defensive player they're assigned to block.

In zone blocking, the linemen all fire out together in one direction. They block anyone in their way, pushing whichever defender they see. Zone blockers are like trains on a track, knocking down everything in their path and not letting anyone cross. A zone blocker's first responsibility is to block defensive linemen. If no defensive lineman is in the way, the offensive lineman can get to the next level, that is, he can race upfield and block a linebacker. One advantage of zone blocking is that no specific offensive player is assigned to get to the next level. Instead, whichever lineman doesn't have anyone to block can be used effectively.

Traps and Pulls

If linemen blocked the same way on every play, the defense would know exactly how to avoid them to make tackles. Traps and pulls are ways for the offense to change strategy to surprise the defense. Guards are usually assigned to trap and pull, but tackles and the center can run these plays just as well.

Imagine a defensive lineman is very fast, so fast that he sometimes beats the offensive player assigned to block him. What can the offense do? Let him get past the offensive line surge. Let the defender think he's going to make a play, but send the tackle from the other side of the field to run behind the line

Can You Find the Traps and Pulls?

Now that you know a bit about how linemen play, you can look closely for a pulling guard or a trapping tackle. Each time you notice one of these plays, write down what you saw, whether the lineman made the block he was supposed to make, and how many yards the play gained.

right toward where the defender will be. This tackle blocks the defender sideways and out of the play. Such a play is called a trap because the defender is usually surprised and can't see the tackle coming.

Another way to trick the defense is to pull a guard or tackle into a hole. When the offensive line creates a hole for a running back to run through, the defensive linebackers are coached to get in that hole to stop the running back. To trick the defense, the offense sends the guard from the other side of the field to run into the hole ahead of the running back. The guard blocks the linebacker who thinks he's going to make a play, and the running back can keep running.

Pass Protection

Passing plays are a bit simpler for linemen. Instead of creating a surge, their job is to keep the defenders away from the quarterback. They form a pocket by pushing the rushers forward and to the side. Sometimes the linemen have to stand their ground against a big, strong, bullrushing defensive lineman. Sometimes, though, it's good enough just to make the defender go away from the quarterback. On passing plays, all that matters is that the quarterback has enough time to throw. Whether defenders are knocked down or merely pushed aside is not important.

The major difficulty in pass protection is picking up a blitz. When the defense sends five or six players, the quarterback is supposed to notice this and throw to the hot receiver. The line still has to give him enough time to make that throw. It's usually most important to block the players coming up the middle, because they can get to the quarterback fastest. A tackle who sees a blitz might have to leave his man to help out the guard and center. Often, the running back is assigned to help out the offensive line on a blitz—he can block the outside guy that the tackle let go.

Hide the Football

There are ten football words hiding in these sentences. Can you find them all? We've given you a list of words to look for, but watch out—there are extra words in the list!

BLOCK	FOULS	LINE	PUNT	SNAP
CANTER	FUMBLE	PIGSKIN	RUSH	SWEEP
CLOCK	KICK	PLAY	SCORE	TEAM

1. Is the game on one disc or eleven cassettes?

2. We won! Hear us "Hooray!"

3. The champ lay winded in the end zone.

4. The quarterback spun, then threw the ball.

5. Tired players nap before a big game.

6. Don't panic! Lock the stadium door!

7. All I need is to move the ball four more yards!

8. Losing teams weep in private.

9. All of Ray Spigs' kin came to watch him play!

10. Drinking iced tea makes players less thirsty.

Big Excitement: The Tackle-Eligible Play

On virtually every play, the linemen do nothing but block. In fact, because they line up in the middle of the formation on the line of scrimmage, the linemen aren't even eligible to catch a pass.

Once in a while, though, a strange formation can put an offensive tackle on the end of the line of scrimmage. Then, the tackle is an eligible receiver for that play. The tackle can pretend to block, then run out for a pass. Especially if this is done near the end zone, the defense can be taken completely by surprise. A quick pass to the wide-open tackle can score an easy touchdown. The tackle-eligible play is very rare. Even Anthony Muñoz only scored four touchdowns in his whole career.

If you plan on playing offensive line for your high school, don't get your hopes up of catching a pass on a tackle-eligible play. The play is illegal under high school rules. You'll have to make it to the NFL to catch a pass as a lineman.

In the NFL Today

Center Jeff Saturday runs the offensive line for one of the best offensive teams in the NFL. He played at the University of North Carolina but was not selected in the NFL draft. In 1999, he joined the Indianapolis Colts. The Colts' Peyton Manning-led offense makes all kinds of adjustments at the line of scrimmage. As the center, it is Jeff's job to be sure that the blocking scheme is set for whatever Peyton calls. It requires amazing mental toughness for Jeff to think through and communicate the necessary information, knowing that he's about to be rammed by the 300-pound defensive tackle crouched in front of him. Jeff received the prestigious Tuesday Morning Quarterback Non-QB Non-RB NFL MVP award in 2007, and he has been elected to three Pro Bowls.

Walter Payton Embodies . . . the Running Back

It may seem obvious, but the running back's job is to take a handoff from the quarterback and run. Yes, you knew that already, right? The running back has other jobs as well, but by far the most important is to carry the ball.

A good ballcarrier is not only fast but is also quick and able to change directions on the spur of the moment. Strong running backs can make correct decisions about where to run the ball. When the offensive line is zone blocking, it's not clear right away exactly where the best spot to run will be. The running back has to read his blocks. For example, a zone running play might be designed to get the ball outside, toward the sideline. But if the outside defender has pushed outside to stop this play, the running back has to recognize right away to cut straight up the field or back to the middle, wherever the line has opened up space.

Beyond speed, quickness, and decision-making, the running back has to be tough. The running back probably is tackled more times per game than anyone else. A runner who can still gain a few yards after getting hit by a defender is extremely valuable. If the running back can bounce right up, ready to carry the ball again on the next play, he's making an enormous contribution to the offense.

What else does a running back have to do besides run? First of all, he often has to block on passing plays. Especially if the defense sends a blitz, the running back has to be aware of any rushers that the offensive line might miss.

A Favorite Fantasy Player

LaDainian Tomlinson graduated from Texas Christian University, where he led the NCAA in rushing both his junior and senior seasons. The San Diego Chargers chose him in the first round of the 2001 draft. He dominated

WORDS to KNOW

ELIGIBLE RECEIVERS: On every play, the offense must line up seven players on the line of scrimmage. The middle five of these players may not catch a pass. Only players on the end of this line are eligible receivers. Players who line up behind the line of scrimmage are eligible receivers.

Football GREAT

Walter Payton

Walter "Sweetness" Payton played for thirteen years, from 1975–1987. In 1975, the Bears drafted him with their first pick. Walter set eight NFL records in his career, including the most rushing yards in a single game, most career rushing yards, and most career total yards. Walter Payton remains perhaps the most loved Bear in recent history.

the NFL the same way he did his college opponents. An outstanding running back generally gains at least 1,000 yards in a season and averages just over four yards per carry. LaDainian has rushed for 1,200 or more yards every year, including his rookie year, with an overall average of 4.5 yards per carry.

LaDainian has scored 115 rushing touchdowns in the first seven years of his career. One aspect of LaDainian's game that makes him extra valuable is his receiving. He's caught more than fifty passes every year, including a 100-catch season in 2003, while still putting up his amazing rushing statistics. LaDainian has even thrown seven touchdown passes! Because he always puts up big numbers, he is often the first player drafted in fantasy football leagues.

Jerry Rice Is . . . the Wide Receiver

The receiver's main job is possibly the simplest to understand: get open, catch the ball, and then run with the ball.

Get Open

On each passing play, a receiver is assigned a route to run. The route tells the receiver which way to run and when to change directions. The receiver and the quarterback will practice that route hundreds of times, so the quarterback will have an idea of when and where to throw the ball. It's the receiver's job to run the route full speed, the same way he ran it in practice, to make it easier for the quarterback to read whether the receiver is open.

Depending on the defense, sometimes a receiver has to adjust the route. For example, it's a bad idea to run right into a defender's zone (an area of the field the defender is responsible for), because then the receiver would be covered easily. Against a zone defense, the receiver might need to stop his route early to stay open. On the other hand, against a man-to-man defense, the receiver should keep running past his defender or he might need to adjust his route away from his defender.

Catch the Ball

This may sound like on obvious skill not even worthy of mention. But there's nothing that's more frustrating to an offense than the perfect pass thrown to an open receiver who drops the ball. On the other hand, there's nothing more exciting or inspiring than an outstanding catch. A receiver must work to develop good hands—yes, hands—because the ball should always be caught with the hands, not cradled against the body. Receivers can practice diving for a catch or catching balls that are thrown off target or with a lot of force. The more experience someone has catching difficult passes, the more likely that person is to make the tough catch in the game.

Run!

As soon as the receiver catches the ball, he must tuck the ball away like a running back. Ball security should be first priority. Then he has to get that ball upfield. A receiver who has caught the ball is usually far away from the biggest defenders. If he can beat one or two tacklers, he might score a touchdown.

Blocking

Even the best receivers don't get the ball thrown to them more than ten or so times per game. Truly great receivers help their team win on every play.

On running plays, a receiver will usually have a blocking assignment. No, he won't have to block that 320-pound nose tackle, but he might have to block a linebacker or safety so the running back can run toward the sideline. Receivers should learn proper blocking form, especially because they often weigh less than people they're supposed to block. Fortunately, it's not necessary to knock a defender down on every play. Just getting in the way and making some physical contact is

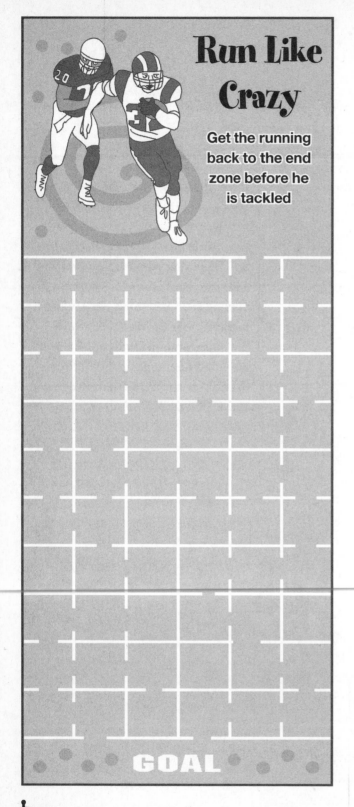

Run Like Crazy

Get the running back to the end zone before he is tackled

GOAL

often enough. But the stronger a blocker you are, the farther away from you a cornerback might play, letting you take advantage of him on a passing play!

Peyton's Target

Wide receiver Marvin Harrison was a first-round pick in 1996. He has played more than a decade for the Indianapolis Colts, mostly as Peyton Manning's primary receiver. Prior to the 2007 season, in which he only played five games due to an injury, Marvin's durability had been outstanding. Before 2007 he played in 170 games over eleven years and missed only six games. In every season since 1999 and before 2007 he gained more than 1,000 yards receiving with double-digit touchdown catches. Marvin's skill, work ethic, team leadership, and statistics all demonstrate him to be the best receiver in the NFL. Yet he's one of the few top receivers who doesn't feel the need to show off. When he scores a touchdown, he doesn't dance or talk trash at the defender he beat. He just tosses the ball to the referee, knowing that he's been in the end zone before and he'll be back soon.

A Receiver Who Returns

Devin Hester of the Bears was a rookie defensive back in 2006, but he made his mark with an NFL record: six special teams touchdowns—two on kickoff returns, three on punt returns, and one on a 108-yard return of a missed field goal. Devin was just as successful in 2007. He led the NFL with four punts and two kickoffs returned for touchdowns. The Bears made him a wide receiver, and he scored a touchdown on a pass from quarterback Brian

The EVERYTHING KIDS' Football Book

Griese in a game against the Vikings. In the same game, Devin returned a punt eighty-nine yards for a touchdown.

Offensive Schemes: Formations and Methods of Attack

Way back at the beginning of football, the rules didn't allow forward passes. Every play had to be a running play. The defense had an easier time because there was no need to defend the deep part of the field.

Single-Wing Formation

Even after the forward pass was made legal from anywhere behind the line of scrimmage in 1933, football still was a running game. Plays were designed for blockers to open holes for running backs. In the single-wing formation, the stack of two wingbacks (running backs positioned behind an end) and a fullback (a running back mainly used as a blocker) helped the offensive linemen block. The quarterback took the snap five yards in the backfield and usually ran behind his blockers on the strong side of the formation.

T Formation

The T formation became widespread beginning in the late 1930s. In the T, the quarterback took the snap under center with his running backs behind him. This was an improvement over the single wing because the quarterback could hand off to any of the running backs, which meant the defense couldn't predict who would carry the ball. Furthermore, passing became easier in the T. If the quarterback faked a handoff, he would be in a good position to throw a pass.

The Passing Game

As passing became a more important part of offensive football, receivers (called split ends or flankers)

FUN FACT

Receivers Win the Game with Blocking!

Late in the 1988 AFC championship game, the Cincinnati Bengals were driving for a touchdown against the Buffalo Bills. A fifteen-yard penalty saved the Bengals' drive and gave them the winning score. What happened? Well, all day long the Bengals receivers had been blocking hard on every running play, even when the play was not in their direction. All these blocks were clean but tough. Finally, one of the Bills defenders got mad and shoved the Bengals receiver after the play, earning a penalty and allowing the Bengals to score a touchdown.

WORDS to KNOW

LATERAL: The rules about forward passes are very strict. But any player can throw a backward pass at any time. A backward pass is called a lateral.

began lining up farther away from the center. This forced the defense to move players away from the middle of the field to cover the receivers, opening up the running game as well as the passing game. The modern pro set eventually evolved from the T formation: two running backs behind the quarterback (under center), a tight end (part lineman, part receiver, the tight end lines up next to the tackle but is eligible to receive a pass), a flanker, and a wide receiver.

Option Offense

When a team has an athletic quarterback who has not developed into a first-rate passer, they might choose to run an option offense. In this run-based offense, the quarterback runs, intending to pitch the ball to a running back who trails behind him. If the defense covers the running back, though, the quarterback has the option to keep the ball and run upfield himself. Many college teams of the 1960s and 1970s used the wishbone offense in which three running backs gave the quarterback a triple option. Option offenses may only throw three or four passes per game, but these are often so surprising to the defense that they result in long gains.

West Coast Offense

In high-level college football and in the NFL, usually the quarterback is not the best athlete on the field but instead is a deadly accurate thrower and an excellent decision maker. The goal of these offenses is for the quarterback to evaluate the defense and get the ball to a great athlete where he has room to run. For example, the West Coast offense is a passing offense but one that pays more attention to short than long passes. The strategy is to throw the ball quickly to open receivers five to ten yards downfield. These receivers can sometimes break for long runs after the catch. Even if they can't, eventually defenders can be fooled into allowing a deep pass or a long run.

Run-and-Shoot Offense

Some teams took the West Coast offense a step farther: they lined up four or five receivers on every play and only rarely ran the ball. This was called the run-and-shoot offense and was popular in the late 1980s and early 1990s. The Houston Oilers with quarterback Warren Moon and the Detroit Lions with running back Barry Sanders were the most famous run-and-shoot teams. But unless your running back was as good as Barry Sanders at breaking tackles, the run-and-shoot could be stopped by an athletic and disciplined defense.

Spread Offense

Today, many college teams have found success with a different kind of run-and-shoot: the spread offense. A spread team usually lines up a running back and a shotgun quarterback—a quarterback who lines up several yards behind the center to receive the snap—in the backfield, and four receivers line up across the field far apart from each other. Because the receivers and even the linemen are spread out so far along the line of scrimmage, the defense also has to spread out. The quarterback can decide who to throw the ball to or whether to run the ball by recognizing how the defense has lined up and reading how the defense reacts to the start of the play.

No NFL team uses a true spread offense because NFL defensive players are simply too fast. A pro offense often has to fool the defense by disguising what they're trying to do. If they can make a defender take even one step the wrong way, they can manage a big gain. Nowadays NFL teams use multiple formations. They might run the same pass to their best receiver several times in a game. But if that receiver starts each play in a different spot on the field, the defense never knows what to expect.

TRY THIS

The West Coast Offense on the Playground
It's exciting to make long gains, but when the defense knows the quarterback is going to throw deep they can usually break up the pass. Next time you're quarterback, try running a West Coast offense. Throw quick, short passes and let the receivers run with the ball. You'll end up frustrating the defense, and you'll probably win the game.

Fooling the Defense

Skilled players combined with an effective offensive system make it possible for a team to be successful. To make that system work, especially against an equally skilled defense, an offense must occasionally trick the defense. Sometimes that trickery is obvious to everyone when it happens, as when the quarterback fakes a handoff and throws the ball instead. But just as often a play works because of an acting job by a player you may not have noticed, like a receiver who pretends to block before running a pass route, or a tight end who falls down only to get up to catch a pass.

A defense isn't tricked easily. The offense must set up their trickery by establishing patterns that they can later break. For example, a wide receiver might run a post pattern (a route that angles toward the goal post) on each of the first fifteen passing plays, even if the quarterback doesn't throw to that receiver. The defense might get used to covering that post pattern. But on the sixteenth play, the receiver might fake the post and instead run toward the sideline deep downfield. Chances are because they've expected the post, the defenders won't be able to react right away and the receiver will be wide open for a long gain or a touchdown.

A critical part of fooling the defense, then, happens on the plays when there's no fooling. A receiver must run hard on every play, even when he knows he's not going to get the ball. Linemen have to use the same stance for every play. They have to be careful not to give away whether they'll be pass blocking or run blocking. A real handoff should look the same as a fake handoff—the running back should run toward the line of scrimmage, and the quarterback should prepare to pass, no matter who actually has the ball. If all eleven players on a team do their jobs, then a few times in every game the offense should be able to make huge gains on tricky plays.

The EVERYTHING KIDS' Football Book

Chapter 7

DEFENSIVE FOOTBALL

Defense! Defense!

Watch Ray Lewis wrestle a running back to the ground, Michael Strahan burst past the offensive linemen to take down a quarterback, and Asante Samuel snatch a ball out of the air for an interception. They make it look easy, but all three of these defensive players have the smarts to read the offense's plays and the physical strength to make sure they don't succeed.

The Basics

The eleven defensive players line up opposite the offense with one mission—keep the offense from scoring. At first, defensive strategy seems much simpler than offensive strategy: just tackle anyone who tries to run the ball while covering the receivers to be sure they can't catch a pass. But since the offense is always trying to confuse and trick the defense, the defense must disguise who covers whom, and they must adjust their strategies from play to play so they don't become predictable.

Keys to Successful Defense

Regardless of the specific scheme a team runs, the defense uses three kinds of players: defensive linemen, linebackers, and the cornerbacks and safeties who together are called the secondary. In this chapter you'll first learn about the jobs done by each of these positions, then you'll find a discussion of the 4-3 and the 3-4 defenses and how they differ. You'll learn how zone defenses work. When you've read this chapter, you'll be able to understand most of what the announcers at a football game are talking about when they describe a team's defense.

Mean Joe Greene Anchors . . . the Defensive Line

Teams use either three or four defensive linemen. The biggest and strongest of these players line up in the middle of the formation, across from the center and the guards. These are called the defensive tackles. The player who lines up directly across from the center is the nose tackle. The tackles have only one job, but it's an important one: give a couple of offensive linemen someone to block. If two offensive players have to block one defensive lineman, then the other defensive players have a better chance of making a play.

Every defensive tackle tries to make two blockers block him so as to free up space for his linebackers to make a tackle. Mean Joe Greene's rush was so powerful and his alignment so unpredictable that he would often take up three blockers. Under his leadership the Steelers Steel Curtain defense dominated the league for at least a decade.

The defensive linemen on the outside of the formation are called the defensive ends. On running plays, they have a similar job to the defensive tackles: if they can't make the play themselves, they try to occupy two blockers so that someone else is free to tackle the ball-carrier. On passing plays, though, the defensive ends have a one-track mind: get the quarterback. Ideally, they'll tackle the quarterback for a sack. If they can't, they need to hurry the quarterback and make him throw a pass before he's ready. Sometimes the defensive ends can put their arms up and knock down a pass. In any case, the defensive ends must be fast and quick to get around the offensive linemen blocking them and to get to the quarterback as soon as possible. The sooner they bother the quarterback, the shorter the time that the secondary has to cover the receivers and the more likely it is that a quarterback will throw an incomplete or intercepted pass.

Defensive end Jason Taylor has been the best player on the Miami Dolphins defensive line for a decade. The Dolphins have been known to line him up in a different spot on each play in order to force the offense to adjust to block him. Jason has sacked a quarterback more than

Football GREAT

Mean Joe Greene
North Texas State University's sports teams are nicknamed the Mean Green. When Charles Edward Greene showed up in the late 1960s, everyone called him Mean Joe Greene. Joe carried this name with him to the Pittsburgh Steelers, where he played defensive tackle for thirteen seasons and helped his team win four Super Bowls. He was NFL defensive player of the year twice, went to eight Pro Bowls, and was named to the NFL All-Pro team four times.

Purple People Eaters
The Minnesota Vikings went to four Super Bowls in the 1960s and 1970s. They were known as a dominant team during that time, largely due to their awe-inspiring defensive line: tackles Alan Page, Gary Larsen, and Doug Sutherland and ends Carl "Moose" Eller and Jim Marshall. Their motto was "meet at the quarterback." This defensive line earned the nickname the Purple People Eaters. To a quarterback they must have looked like an enormous chewing monster in the Vikings' purple uniforms.

Football GREAT

Mike Singletary

Mike Singletary played for twelve seasons as the Chicago Bears middle linebacker and made the Pro Bowl team ten times. With Mike Singletary in the middle of the defense, the Bears used a new, aggressive defense called the 46. The idea was to blitz all the time and from all different directions. The pinnacle of his career came in the 1985 season, when his top-rated defense led the Bears to a victory in Super Bowl XX. Mike recovered two fumbles in that game in which the defense only allowed a field goal and a very late touchdown in a 46-10 blowout.

100 times in his career. He has scored seven times, a record for a defensive player, and it doesn't seem like Jason is done scoring points. In a game early in the 2007 season, the Dolphins lined him up as a wide receiver and threw the ball to him in the end zone! He didn't score, but he drew a penalty that led to a score on the next play.

Mike Singletary as a . . . Linebacker

The first job of a linebacker is to stop the run. At the snap, they all take a read step toward the line of scrimmage. While they step, they watch the offensive linemen. If the offensive linemen block for a running play, then the read step gives the linebacker momentum to fill whatever gap opens up for the running back to come through. It's the linebacker's job to run wherever he has to go to stop the running back. That means watching the backfield to know who has the ball. It also means using his hands to keep offensive players from blocking him.

If the linemen set up to pass block, then the linebackers drop back into pass coverage. Most of the time, linebackers will be responsible for stopping receivers who run short routes across the field. Sometimes a linebacker will be assigned to watch the running back in case he comes out of the backfield to catch a pass. The specific coverage assignment depends on the team's defensive strategy. That strategy may well include linebacker blitzes, where a linebacker rushes the quarterback once he reads a pass play.

Communication

The linebackers serve key roles as communicators for the defense. Before the snap, the defensive linemen don't have a good view of the offensive formation

Most Valuable Player

What kind of football career will this player have? To figure out what the coach tells him, fill in the blanks with the numbered words.

Hey, Coach!

I want to

play 1 _____,

2 _____,

and 3 _____!

OK — 4 _____ at the

1 _____ of

the 7 _____,

2 _____ the

6 _____ 8 _____,

and 3 _____

9 _____ who gets

5 _____ it!

6 WATER

7 BENCH

1 END

4 SIT

2 GUARD

5 NEAR

3 TACKLE

8 BUCKET

9 ANYONE

because they are trying to get in a low-to-the-ground stance. The linebackers have to tell them what they see: which is the strong side of the offense where there are more players? How many runners are in the backfield? Should the defense change its strategy? The linebackers will usually communicate this information using some sort of code words so the offense can't catch on.

Making the Tackle

More than anyone else on the defense, the linebackers are in charge of tackling. The defensive linemen try to force the running back to where the linebackers can make a tackle. A good linebacker is not only fast enough to get where he's supposed to be, but he's strong, too, with outstanding tackling form: head up, legs driving, arms wrapping the ballcarrier in a bear hug as he falls to the ground. Sure, all defensive players should be good tacklers, but the linebackers have to be the best.

A New Bear

Linebacker Brian Urlacher played four seasons for the University of New Mexico before the Bears made him their number one draft pick in 2000. He started at middle linebacker through most of his first year, and that's where he's stayed ever since. His success at that position, where he makes ten to fifteen tackles per game and covers the field like a monster, reminds fans of Chicago legend Mike Singletary. Brian's strength (he set weightlifting records in college) allows him to take on and defeat the blocks of big offensive lineman. That makes it difficult to run on him. Brian's excellent speed allows him to cover the deep middle of the field. Because he is so good in coverage, the Bears safeties can focus on the receivers on the sides of the field, knowing that Brian has the middle taken care of. Brian played in the Super Bowl for the first time after the 2006 season, making ten tackles in a loss to the Colts.

FUN FACT

Help from the Sideline

As soon as it's clear whether a play is a running or passing play, every player on the sideline yells "Run!" or "Pass!" On a passing play, as soon as the quarterback throws the ball, the sideline yells "Ball!" Linebackers and defensive backs make their own reads, but they can and do use the sideline's call to help them out.

The EVERYTHING KIDS' Football Book

Darrell Green Covers His Man in . . . the Secondary

Together, the cornerbacks and safeties are called defensive backs or the secondary. Whereas the first job of the linebackers is to stop the run, the first job of the defensive backs is to cover receivers.

The Safeties

The safeties line up deep in the backfield, ten to fifteen yards from the line of scrimmage. The strong safety lines up to the tight end's side of the formation, while the free safety lines up opposite the strong safety. At the snap, the safeties watch the tight end and the other linemen to quickly find out whether the play will be a run or pass. On a running play, the safeties, especially the strong safety, come toward the line in run support. They aid the linebackers in bringing down running backs. Safeties are usually a bit less aggressive in plugging holes because they are the last line of defense. If a linebacker misses a tackle, he's got more help behind him, but if a safety gets out of position, he costs a touchdown.

The safety's main job, though, is pass coverage. The safety is usually responsible for a deep zone. Once the safety recognizes a passing play, he finds the receiver most likely to threaten his area of the field—that's usually the tight end or the slot receiver (the receiver lined up between the last player on the offensive line and the wide receiver). The safety reads this receiver's route, preparing to cover him if he stays in the safety's zone.

The safety can't focus exclusively on this one player, though. At the same time he has to be aware of what the outside receiver is doing, even though the outside receiver is at first the cornerback's responsibility. If two receivers run crossing routes, the safety and cornerback must notice, and they should switch coverage, with the safety taking the deeper route.

WORDS to KNOW

CROSSING ROUTES: In a zone defense, defenders cover an area of the field. Crossing routes try to confuse the defenders about which receivers are in their area. A simple set of crossing routes could have the receivers cut in front of one another, trading sides of the field. Or a receiver could start on a deep route but pull up short while his teammate runs by him into the deep zone.

ON AN ISLAND: A cornerback is often responsible for covering the same receiver through most of the game. The corner will have help from a safety for many plays, but sometimes he will be in true man-on-man coverage. In that case, the cornerback is said to be "on an island"—he's all alone, far away from anyone else, with no help in sight.

Safeties aren't always in a deep zone. A safety could be part of double coverage on a dangerous receiver. He could be asked to scoot up to stop a team that's been running a lot, leaving pass coverage to the cornerbacks and the other safety. Or he could rush the quarterback on a safety blitz. The safety has to be an athletic player to fill all of these roles.

The Cornerbacks

Cornerbacks line up on the corners of the formation, in front of the widest receivers. Corners will help out on running plays, usually by attempting to force a ballcarrier back to the inside where the linebackers are waiting for him. Yet the cornerbacks must play the pass first. If the cornerback makes the mistake of looking to see whether the quarterback handed off, his receiver will run by him. The general rule for cornerbacks is to defend as if the quarterback will throw the ball until the sideline calls "Run!"

A cornerback always has to know where his safeties are supposed to be. For example, are the corners supposed to cover short routes, with the safeties playing deep? Or will the safety cover inside routes, with the corner taking the outside and deep routes? Knowing where the safeties are will tell the cornerback how to cover a receiver. The cornerback should cover any route that the safety won't be able to get to.

Jamming the Receiver

Passing offenses rely on precise routes and practiced timing between the quarterback and receivers. One of the best ways to disrupt an offense is for the cornerbacks to jam the receivers right after the snap. In high school and college, defenders can bump a receiver until the ball is thrown. Unless the cornerback is supposed to cover the deep part of the field, it's useful to give the receiver a bump. But if the cornerback misses when he tries to jam, the receiver could be wide open.

The EVERYTHING KIDS' Football Book

The Two Major Defensive Alignments

Most teams organize their defense in one of two ways. The 3-4 defense uses three defensive linemen and four linebackers, while the 4-3 defense uses four defensive linemen and three linebackers. There are advantages and disadvantages to each. Most of the time, the choice of which scheme to use depends on the players a team has to fill the positions.

The majority of NFL teams use the 4-3. Four linemen make it easier to keep the offensive line busy. Even though there are only three linebackers, they are more likely to be free to make a play. In a 4-3, each of the three linebackers has his own job:

- The strong-side linebacker, called "Sam," lines up on the tight end's side of the field. Since the offense is more likely to run toward the tight end, Sam is likely to be the person in place to stop a running back.
- The weak-side linebacker, called "Will," lines up opposite the tight end. He has to be a bit faster than Sam, because he more often has to cross the whole field to make a play. Since Will is pretty fast, he is used in pass coverage more often than Sam.
- The middle linebacker, called "Mike," is the captain of the defense. He is usually the player who communicates with the coaches and then runs the huddle to tell his teammates the play. Mike's position in the middle lets him read running plays quickly. By seeing where the ballcarrier is probably headed, Mike can often be the first one there to make the tackle. A speedy middle linebacker is often used in pass coverage. Especially when the two safeties are sitting in deep coverage, the Mike linebacker has to be ready to cover the tight end over the middle of the field.

A 3-4 defense uses these same three linebackers, plus one more inside linebacker. Usually on pass plays,

FUN FACT

Heisman Winner
Only one defensive player has ever won college football's coveted Heisman Trophy—Michigan cornerback Charles Woodson in 1997. He beat out a strong field that included Tennessee quarterback Peyton Manning and Marshall wide receiver Randy Moss. Charles was drafted by the Oakland Raiders and was named the 1998 Defensive Rookie of the Year.

Zone Blitz

In a zone blitz, a linebacker rushes the quarterback, but one of the defensive linemen doesn't rush. Instead, the lineman drops back in pass coverage, taking over the linebacker's responsibilities. The zone blitz can confuse the quarterback into throwing an interception. But you could argue that a zone blitz isn't even a blitz! Only four players rush the quarterback.

one of the four linebackers will rush the quarterback with the defensive linemen. An advantage of the 3-4 is that the offensive line never knows which linebacker will be rushing.

Defensive Strategies

The scheme, whether 4-3 or 3-4, is a description of how a team lines up and what roles each player fills. All defenses, regardless of their overall scheme, use pass rushing strategies, while the secondary uses man and zone coverage, sometimes in combination.

Blitz!

In playground football, a player who doesn't count to seven before rushing the quarterback is said to blitz. The number of blitzes are limited to, say, once every four downs. Since regular football does not require the defense to count before rushing, the term blitz takes on a different meaning.

A defense normally sends four players to rush the quarterback. These are the four defensive linemen. In a 3-4 defense, it's the three linemen and (usually) the Sam linebacker. In a blitz, a fifth or even a sixth player rushes the quarterback. That's all there is to it.

The obvious advantage of sending a blitz is that the offensive line is outnumbered, so the quarterback has less time to throw a pass before he's tackled. But at the same time, the defense has left fewer players to cover the receivers. If the quarterback does manage to throw a pass, a blitz makes it much easier to find an open receiver who can run a long way after he catches the ball.

The most common blitz technique calls for a linebacker to rush in between two defensive linemen. A safety can also blitz, and he can get more of a running start because he lines up farther from the line of scrimmage, but it will take him a bit longer to reach the quarterback and make it extra difficult to cover the

Words to Play By

Place all the letters into their proper spaces in the empty grid. You will see that this familiar saying is true both on and off the football field!

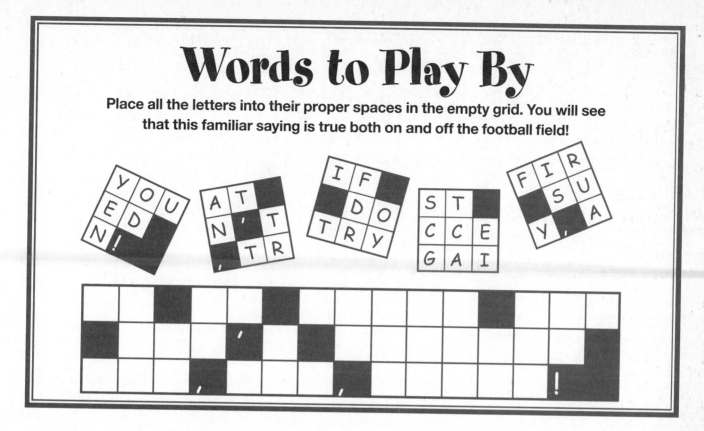

receivers. Occasionally you'll even see a corner blitz, when a cornerback lines up as if to cover a receiver but instead sprints toward the quarterback at the snap.

Stunt

The stunt is a way to confuse the offensive linemen. Normally, the defensive linemen and linebackers rush straight ahead, trying to get into a gap between offensive players. In a stunt, two linemen or linebackers trade places so that they don't attack straight ahead. For example, the nose tackle might run outside the defensive end, hoping that the offense can't figure out who should block him. In that case, a linebacker or another defensive lineman would probably move to cover the area where the nose tackle is normally supposed to be.

A stunt is a bit of a gamble. If the offense doesn't adjust, the stunt can lead to a sack or a tackle for a huge loss. But if the offense recognizes the stunt and knows what to do about it, they might be able to take advantage for a big gain.

Different Types of Zone Defense

On most passing plays, the defensive backs will play zone coverage. The most common basic zone defense is called the cover 2. In this scheme, the safeties play deep and each is in charge of half the width of the field, while the cornerbacks and linebackers defend against short passes. If you're watching a game, you can recognize the cover 2 by watching where the defensive backs line up at the snap. The two safeties will both be about fifteen yards downfield, and the cornerbacks will play close to the wide receivers.

One disadvantage to the cover 2 is that the offense has an easier time running the ball because both safeties are so far back. If the defense needs to change strategy to stop the run, they can switch to the cover 3. In this scheme, the strong safety plays close to the line of

The **EVERYTHING KIDS'** Football Book

scrimmage, while the deep part of the field is split into three zones for the free safety and the two cornerbacks. To recognize cover 3, look for a single deep safety. The cornerbacks will play five yards or so away from the receivers so that they can get to their deep third of the field.

Though cover 2 and cover 3 are the zones you will see most frequently, there are lots of other coverage strategies. To guard against the deep pass, the defensive backs each cover one-fourth of the field. On the other hand, a defense might play straight man-to-man, usually when they send a big blitz. Man-to-man defense is only effective if the rushers get to the quarterback very quickly. To give some protection against the deep pass in man-to-man coverage, one safety could play deep while everyone else covers a man. This is called cover 1.

The Specialists: Kickers, Punters, and Blocking the Kick

You might think that the kicking team would be considered part of the offense. Perhaps it should be, as they are trying to score points. However, the kicking unit, as well as the players who return kicks, are considered separate from both offense and defense. Kick and kick return units are called the special teams. Usually, especially in college and the NFL, players on the special teams are not starters on offense or defense. These units have special, separate practice time. Watch a game closely. When it's time for a punt or a field goal, you'll see mass substitutions as the special teams run onto the field.

The Kickoff

On a kickoff, the kicking team not only has to kick the ball way down the field, but they also have to tackle anyone who tries to return the kick. The techniques used by members of the kicking team are similar to those of a

WORDS to KNOW

TOUCHBACK: The best kickoff results in a touchback. If the kick goes into the end zone, the offense gets the ball at the twenty-yard line. If the ball doesn't go into the end zone, usually the kick returner can get past the twenty.

COFFIN CORNER: The best possible punt will go out of bounds but will not get into the end zone for a touchback. Punters often practice aiming their punts so they'll go out of bounds inside the five yard line. Such a punt is called a coffin corner punt.

defense: avoid blocks, get in position, and make a tackle. Positioning is even more important on a kickoff than on a regular play because the players are so spread out. When a kick returner catches the ball, he can usually run ten to fifteen yards before he comes anywhere near a tackler. The tacklers have to run very fast and stay away from blockers until they get near the returner. Then they have to position themselves so the returner can't get away. A tackle on a kickoff usually isn't made by one person flying full speed in the open field. It's usually made by a whole bunch of tacklers closing in until they can make the play together.

Good kickoffs go high, deep, and toward one side of the field. The higher the kick, the longer the kicking team has to run down the field to get in the right position. By kicking to one side, the kicking team reduces the amount of field they have to cover. But the kicker has to be careful. If the kick goes out of bounds, the return team gets the ball in good field position.

At the same time that the kicking team tries to tackle the kick returner, the members of the return team are trying to block for the returner. Blocking on a kick return is more difficult than on a regular play. Positioning is incredibly important. A blocker tries to get in between the defender and the returner to push the defender away. That's harder than it sounds because the defenders are all running as fast as they can. It's unlikely that a blocker will knock anyone down; rather, blockers try to push, shove, and use their hands to make the defender go the wrong way.

The Punt

The kicking, tackling, and return strategies for punts are similar to those on kickoffs. There are a few main differences:

The **EVERYTHING KIDS** Football Book

- Before the punting team runs downfield, they have to block to protect the punter. Their most important job is to prevent the punt from being blocked. Only after the punt is kicked should the team race to tackle the returner.
- If a punt goes out of bounds, the receiving team gets the ball right where it left the field. So it's usually a good idea to boom a punt out of bounds—then no one can return it!
- The gunners: Usually the punting team lines up two fast players near the sidelines. These are the gunners, who don't bother protecting the punter. At the snap, the gunners race downfield as if they were in kickoff coverage. Problem is, the return team is allowed to line up right across from the gunners. The gunners have to find a way around one or two players who are trying to bump, push, and hit them. Try watching the gunners next time you see a punt to see the kinds of moves they make to get themselves down the field.

Field Goals and Extra Points

If all goes right, a field goal or an extra point should be routine. The long snapper gets the ball to the holder, who puts the ball down for the kicker to kick. The only reason these plays look easy is that teams practice them over and over and over.

The Long Snapper

On many teams, the long snapper is not the regular center. His primary job is to snap the football back quickly and accurately to the holder. He should block after he lets the snap go, but blocking is far less important than the accuracy of the snap. The long snapper practices snaps for hours each week. In fact, there are special summer camps dedicated just to long snapping skills! Fans rarely see the name of the long snapper, but he's the next most important player on special teams behind the punter or kicker. If a kick goes bad, it's probably because of a less-than-perfect snap.

FUN FACT

Illegal Blocks

It seems like a whole lot of kick returns result in penalties for illegal blocks. Kick return blockers cannot block below the waist or in the back. If they do, the penalty is ten yards from the spot of the illegal block. Therefore, it's better just to let someone make a tackle than to make an illegal block on him.

The Holder

The holder is usually also a team's quarterback or punter. He stoops on one knee, ready to catch the snap and place the ball on the ground. Ideally, he puts the ball straight up and down, with the laces pointing away from the kicker.

The Kicker

Years ago, kickers ran straight up to the ball and kicked it with their toe. In the 1970s, kickers figured out that the ball goes farther if it's kicked from the side, like a soccer player kicks. This kicking technique is called soccer style. Good high school kickers can consistently kick the ball through the uprights from at least thirty to thirty-five yards. In college and in the pros, kickers have to be accurate from much farther away. In fact, NFL kickers routinely hit fifty-yard field goals.

You might have practiced kicking before. If you used a kicking tee and if you approached the ball at a full sprint, you might have been able to kick the ball a long way, maybe even thirty or more yards. So you can kick field goals for a college team, right? Well, you weren't really kicking a field goal. Kicking tees are only allowed for kickoffs, and NFL kickers can kick the ball sixty to eighty yards on a kickoff. For a field goal, the ball must be held on the ground. Making it even more difficult, the kicker has to kick a field goal quickly, before the defense can rush in to block it. The kicker actually starts the run-up to the kick before the holder is holding the ball! On a kickoff, the kicker might run ten to fifteen yards on his run-up, but he only gets about five to seven yards for a field goal.

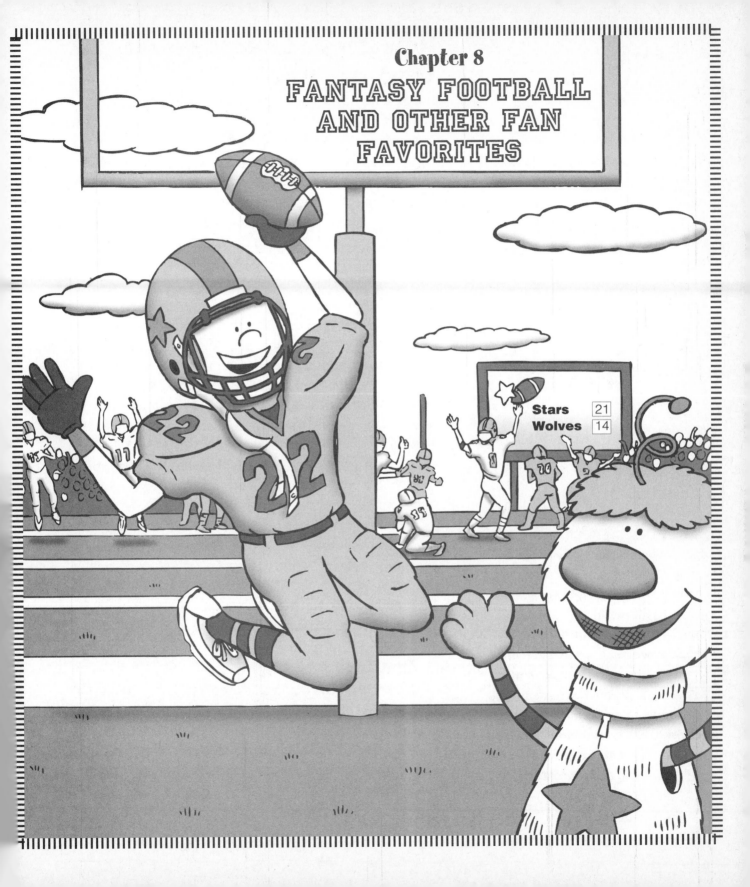

Chapter 8

FANTASY FOOTBALL AND OTHER FAN FAVORITES

How Does a Fantasy League Work Anyway?

Imagine owning a football team. You're the person in charge of everything, from the uniform design to player moves to game strategy. Wouldn't that be great? There's no reason you can't own an NFL franchise someday. All it costs to own a team is about a billion dollars. What? You don't think you'll have a billion dollars to spare anytime soon? The closest substitute for you will be to own a fantasy football team. You won't get a luxury box at an enormous stadium, but you'll still have fun and be in charge.

Fantasy Basics

Fantasy football can be a little complicated, so you should ask a parent to help you. You'll need permission to use the computer too. Each fantasy league has different rules, but they have the same basic idea. You'll choose a number of NFL players to be on your team. Every time one of your players does something good in a game—scores a touchdown, gains yards, kicks a field goal—your team gains points. If your player does something bad, though, like throwing an interception or losing a fumble, your team loses points.

Each weekend your team will play against another team in your league. You'll play one player, or sometimes two players, at each position, and so will your opponent. Add up all the points your players score over their games that weekend. If you score more points than your opponent, you win your fantasy game.

How to Start a League

One of the reasons fantasy football is so intriguing is that the fantasy team owners have to do many of the things that real football team owners do. To start, you have to get a group of owners together to form a league. That's not easy, even for real teams. If you can find an established league to join, that's easiest. But if you can simply find seven or more friends who want to play, then you can create your own league.

Beginning the Season

Once you know who's in the league and who is keeping track of all the league business, you're ready to start. Every season begins with a player draft in which each team takes turns picking players. The most fun way to do this is to conduct a live draft. Get all the owners together at someone's house and start picking. Usually you randomly determine the order that everyone picks in. Put a time limit of about one minute on each pick so that the draft doesn't take all day. Each team should choose enough players to fill its roster plus have a few extra players to substitute in if needed.

After the draft, all the players who weren't picked become available on the waiver wire. If you decide you want to replace one of your drafted players—for example, if someone gets hurt or if you realize that your player is having a bad season—you can drop your player and replace him off of the waiver wire. The rules for waiver pickups are different for every league. In some leagues, teams can just pick up players whenever they feel like it. In other leagues, teams can only make a certain number of pickups. Sometimes teams with better records have to wait for worse teams to make their choices first.

Each week you set your lineup, which means you pick one player at each position to represent your team. You have to pick carefully. If one of your players scores three touchdowns in a game and you left him on the bench that week, you'll feel silly.

Once the games start on Sunday afternoon, you can sit back and watch. Now that you're playing fantasy football, you are doing more than rooting for your favorite NFL team. You're also rooting for all of your players to do well. That means you have a special interest in more than just one game, making the weekend even more festive.

WORDS to KNOW

COMMISSIONER: The commissioner is like the referee of fantasy football, someone who keeps the game running. He or she keeps track of statistics (which usually just means keeping an eye on the Web site that does your stats for you), sets up the rules of the league and the draft, and makes the final decisions if there are disagreements. It's best to find a commissioner who isn't also a team owner, but if there's an owner whom everyone in the league trusts to do the job well, then that's fine.

TRY THIS

Draft Advice

Kickers are the least important position in fantasy football. Sure, some kickers are better than others, but you can always find a starting kicker on the waiver wire who can do nearly as well as the best kicker in the league. Don't draft a kicker until the last round! Use your valuable draft picks on the offensive skill positions first.

Manage Your Fantasy Draft with Skillful Strategy

The strength of the team you draft depends on how much preparation you do. That doesn't mean you have to study obsessively for weeks, checking statistics and predictions fifteen hours a day. You can have a very good draft if you come with two things: a list and a plan.

Make a List of Players

During the draft, you will be under pressure to make very quick decisions about which players to choose. If you've thought ahead of time which players are best, you'll have an easier time during the actual draft.

There are several ways to make your list. One thought is to rank the top 200 or so players in the order you'd want them. Then when it's your turn, you will lean toward taking the highest ranking player left. This sort of list will help the most in the early rounds, when you still need to fill pretty much every position on your roster. Another idea is to make several shorter lists, ranking the top thirty or so players at each position. This sort of list can help the most in later rounds, when you need to fill out every position on your team.

However you make your list, be sure to cross off each player as he's drafted. It can be embarrassing to announce the player you want only to find out that someone already picked him.

Make a Plan

You should be able to find out ahead of time whether you pick first, last, or somewhere in between. Try going through a mock draft, where you pretend to pick players for each team, to guess which players might be available in the first couple of rounds. This process will help you figure out your plan.

The EVERYTHING KIDS' Football Book

You should be able to make a reasonable guess as to who your first choice will be. You might even be able to guess at your second choice too. After that, it's hard to predict which players will be taken. Beyond the second round, you should have a general plan rather than a specific player to go after. For example, if you are sure you will be able to take a star quarterback like Peyton Manning in the first round, you might decide to take three running backs before you even consider finding a backup quarterback. Or you might decide to wait until the fourth or fifth round to select a quarterback if you know you will get better running backs and receivers this way.

Automatic Drafts

A live draft is by far the most fun way to pick your team, but in some leagues it might not be easy to get the owners together for a draft. In that case, the league can let the computer pick everyone's team. All owners submit a list of players ranked in the order they'd like to choose them. The computer goes from team to team, letting each team have the highest-ranked player remaining on their list. Automatic drafts are less fun and they allow for less strategy, but they're quite a lot quicker than live drafts.

Dominate Your Season with Clever Roster Moves

No doubt, the draft is the most important part of the fantasy football season. But you won't have a perfect draft. Some of your players won't be as good as you expected. You probably missed your chance to draft a player who turns out to be a star. That's okay. If you grabbed a few solid players and at least one star in your draft, your team can still be successful as long as you actively manage the team through the season. You have three techniques available to help you win after draft day: choosing your starters, scouring the waiver wire, and making trades.

FUN FACT

Defense! Defense!

In fantasy football leagues, you pick individual offensive players, like Peyton Manning for quarterback and Braylon Edwards for wide receiver. However, you pick an entire team's defensive unit. That means you'll get the Redskins' defense, not just linebacker London Fletcher.

Where to Get Help With Your List

Each summer, you can find many fantasy football magazines and Web sites that provide lists of players like the ones you'll need for your draft. It is easiest to start with a list made by someone else and then to change it around to suit your needs.

No Need for a Spare Kicker

For the same reasons you probably don't want to draft a kicker early, there's usually no need to put a backup kicker on your bench, especially if you're running out of spots on your roster. If your starting kicker gets hurt or if he's on a bye, just drop him and pick up a new kicker. You'll do better in the long run by saving that roster spot for a running back or quarterback.

WORDS to KNOW

BYE: NFL teams play sixteen games over seventeen Sundays. The Sunday when a team doesn't play is called the team's bye week.

Choosing Your Starters

The roster of your fantasy team will usually have more than one player for each position. If your league lets you start one quarterback each week, then you'll probably have an extra quarterback on the bench. That way, if your star quarterback gets hurt or if he's not doing well, you can replace him with your extra quarterback. The same reasoning applies to the other positions as well.

But each week you have to declare which of your players are starting, that is, which players' statistics will count toward your fantasy league for that week's games. You can only start some of your players, with the rest sitting out for the week.

Sometimes the decision of who to start is pretty obvious. If you have, say, Peyton Manning and Joey Harrington, you're going to start Peyton Manning, the guy who's been one of the absolute top scoring quarterbacks in any league for at least four seasons now. On the other hand, if Manning's Colts are on their bye week and not playing, then you'll have to start Harrington.

Other times, though, it isn't clear who you should start. Imagine you have two running backs. One of them is playing against the best run defense in the NFL, and the other is playing against one of the worst defensive teams. Who should you start? In general, you should always play a true star, someone like LaDainian Tomlinson or Marvin Harrison. Beyond the all-pro players, it's often a good idea to start the player whose team plays against the really bad defense.

NFL Injury Words

You certainly don't want to start someone who turns out to be injured. Be sure to read the NFL injury reports before making your decision. The official NFL injury reports are issued the Friday before a Sunday game. A player will be described with one of four words:

Wacky Weather

Use a dark marker to color in all the shapes with the letters H-O-T. When you are finished, you will have the silly answer to the riddle.

WHY DID THE STADIUM GET HOT AFTER THE GAME?

P	D	H	O	T	L	H	L	Y	T	E	B	P	I
I	E	O	G	H	K	O	P	J	O	W	R	E	K
U	Q	T	H	O	U	T	G	K	H	A	E	W	J
Y	A	H	J	T	I	H	T	L	O	Q	B	Q	L
R	S	O	K	H	T	T	H	A	T	O	H	A	P
E	Z	G	L	K	Y	P	D	S	J	M	P	S	Y
W	X	H	H	O	P	T	E	H	K	H	O	X	B
Q	C	A	O	J	R	O	Y	O	L	O	D	Z	N
A	V	C	T	K	E	H	H	T	P	T	H	D	M
S	B	V	H	A	W	T	K	T	V	O	P	F	Z
D	N	F	T	S	S	O	L	O	C	H	O	C	A
E	M	E	G	W	D	K	M	F	X	D	G	V	S
H	O	N	H	H	H	J	H	G	Z	T	R	O	H
O	U	J	T	M	O	W	O	H	A	T	E	H	R
T	H	K	O	H	T	S	T	L	O	O	W	T	T
T	K	M	O	J	H	D	T	P	G	H	S	J	O
H	M	L	H	P	O	R	O	R	N	O	F	O	H
K	L	R	F	R	K	F	Y	E	M	A	R	G	D
O	P	Y	H	O	L	O	H	S	H	H	O	F	H
H	J	P	T	J	Y	H	D	W	J	O	M	D	O
O	K	W	O	T	R	T	O	A	S	T	N	E	T
T	I	E	H	L	E	T	G	Z	W	O	B	R	Y
H	T	Q	O	H	D	O	L	X	Y	O	X	Q	O

All Mixed Up

It can be confusing to be a fan of fantasy football. Fill in the blanks to see one reason why! There are three possible letters you can use in each blank. Be careful—we've given you one extra fantasy letter!

A H U W

Im_gine t__t

_ f_nt_sy

o_ner __s pl_yers

from t_o

different te_ms.

__en bot_ "re_l"

te_ms pl_y e_ch

ot_er, t_e

f_nt_sy o_ner

_ill _ope t__t

bot_ te_ms

score _ lot!

- Probable means the player is virtually certain to play as he normally does.
- Questionable means the player has about a 50/50 chance of playing or sitting out.
- Doubtful means the player has less than a 25 percent chance of playing.
- Out means the player will not play.

You'll discover that teams use these descriptions differently and sometimes unpredictably. It hurts your fantasy team a lot if you start a quarterback who was listed as probable only to see him sit on the bench. But there's nothing you can do then. . . . The best strategy you can use is to play anyone listed as probable, sit anyone who's doubtful, and don't start a questionable player unless you read in a couple of news articles that he's likely to play.

An Example Game

In the Fantasy League of Gentlemen and Gentlewomen, FC Moose Jaw took on the Fighting Coelacanths.

In this league, players get one point for each pass they catch on top of points for yardage and touchdowns. Therefore, wide receivers are more valuable in this league than in leagues that don't award a point per catch. FC Moose Jaw plays Marvin Harrison at receiver alongside Peyton Manning at quarterback. This is a very strong combination, and not only because these two Colts players are among the best available. Since Marvin is Peyton's favorite target, it is likely that Marvin will catch many or most of Peyton's touchdown passes.

The EVERYTHING KIDS· Football Book

Table 8-1 Starting Lineups: FC Moose Jaw Versus the Fighting Coelacanths

Position	Mooses	Points	Coelacanths	Points
QB	Peyton Manning	10	Carson Palmer	4
RB	Jamal Lewis	1	LaDainian Tomlinson	4
WR	Marvin Harrison	10	Torry Holt	17
TE	Todd Heap	13	Antonio Gates	6
K	Neil Rackers	4	Jeff Wilkins	18
DEF	Ravens	6	Bears	16
Total	Mooses	44	Coelacanths	61

You can tell from this game that touchdowns are the most important statistic in fantasy football. Carson Palmer actually threw for thirty more yards than Peyton Manning did, but since Manning threw a touchdown, he scored six more fantasy points. Similarly, Torry Holt and Marvin Harrison both had good receiving days, but Holt had a touchdown.

This game is a perfect example of how fantasy football is sometimes not just about the big stars. Sure, Peyton Manning helped FC Moose Jaw win a lot of games. He usually scored fifteen or twenty points per game. But on this day, Manning wasn't the difference in the game. Rather, it was St. Louis kicker Jeff Wilkins, who had four field goals (three of which earned a bonus for being more than forty yards long) and three extra points.

How to Read a Football Box Score

If you didn't watch a game, a box score can help you figure out what happened and how your favorite players did. If you own a fantasy football team, the box score gives you the information you need to calculate how many points your players scored.

Customize Your League's Scoring

The standard scoring system for most fantasy leagues awards six points for a touchdown and one point for every twenty yards gained. Quarterbacks might get one point for every fifty passing yards. Kickers usually get one point for an extra point and three for a field goal. Defenses usually earn points for turnovers and touchdowns, with bonuses for yardage and points allowed. But you and your league's commissioner can set up your scoring system however you like.

Backfield Buzz

Put the football vocab words in the grid in alphabetical order from top to bottom. When you are finished, read down the shaded column to get the silly answer to the riddle!

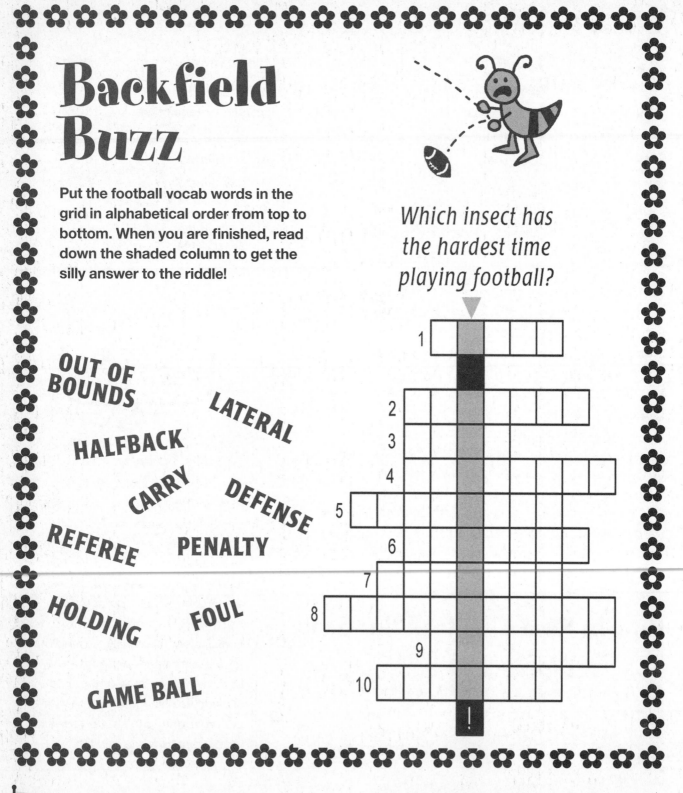

Which insect has the hardest time playing football?

OUT OF BOUNDS

LATERAL

HALFBACK

CARRY

DEFENSE

REFEREE

PENALTY

HOLDING

FOUL

GAME BALL

The EVERYTHING KIDS' Football Book

Decoding the Numbers

Table 8-2 shows the box score from a game between the Ravens and the Chargers. Here's what everything means:

- The top two lines are called the line score: they tell you how many points each team scored in each quarter. From this you can see that the Chargers were winning, 13-7, at halftime, and the Ravens came from behind to win in the fourth quarter!

- Every scoring play is shown next. In the first quarter, Malcom Floyd caught a Philip Rivers pass for thirty-one yards and a touchdown. Nate Kaeding kicked the extra point. The "4:39" means that the touchdown happened four minutes and thirty-nine seconds into the quarter. In the second quarter, you see the two field goals by Nate Kaeding. In the fourth quarter, you see the Baltimore safety.

- You can also see that Baltimore came from behind to win with a late touchdown—this must have been an exciting game! How do you know that? Well, the Ravens scored nine points in the fourth quarter to win by just three. So that last touchdown gave them the lead. And look at the last scoring play. Steve McNair threw a touchdown pass to Todd Heap at 14:26. Since a quarter is fifteen minutes long, the last touchdown was scored with only thirty-four seconds left on the clock. Wow.

- The "A" in the next line stands for attendance. More than 70,000 people showed up in Baltimore to watch the game.

- The team statistics come next. Most of these are pretty clear. The "3rd Down Efficiency" line means the Chargers had third down thirteen times in this game. Of those thirteen tries, only twice did they gain the first down. The Ravens did a bit better, making four first downs in eleven third-down plays. You can see that San Diego

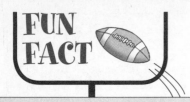

How Do You Tell Who Had a Good Game?

Offensive statistics can't tell you everything about how a player did. For example, the box score doesn't say how many good blocks or broken tackles someone had. However, the stats give you a rough idea of who had a good game. A running back or a receiver who gained 100 yards did very well. Similarly, a quarterback might aim for 300 yards passing with very few interceptions.

had trouble with penalties, losing many more yards than Baltimore.

- The individual stats are where you'll want to look to see how your fantasy players did. Rushing stats tell you the number of carries followed by the total yards gained. LaDainian Tomlinson ran the ball twenty-seven times and gained ninety-eight yards. Receiving stats start with passes caught followed by total yards.

- The passing stats for each quarterback include four numbers. These represent completions, pass attempts, interceptions, and yards gained. Neither quarterback in this game had a huge day. Philip Rivers completed 13 of his 22 passes, throwing one interception and gaining 145 yards. Steve McNair threw a few more completed passes for a few more yards, but he threw two interceptions. Touchdown passes aren't listed here because the list of scoring plays shows them. McNair threw two touchdowns, and Rivers threw one.

How to Find Out More

Newspapers love box scores because they can tell you so much about a game, yet they don't take much space at all to print. The paper can put all of a day's box scores on

Table 8-2

Baltimore Ravens 16, San Diego Chargers 13

San Diego 7 6 0 0 — 13

Baltimore 7 0 0 9 — 16

First Quarter

       SD—M.Floyd 31 pass from P.Rivers (N.Kaeding kick), 4:39.

       Bal—D.Wilcox 5 pass from S.McNair (M.Stover kick), 9:32.

Second Quarter

       SD—FG N.Kaeding 34, 0:09.

       SD—FG N.Kaeding 54, 13:09.

Third Quarter—no scoring

Fourth Quarter

      Bal—Safety, M.Scifres tackled by E.Reed in end zone, 11:28.

      Bal—T.Heap 10 pass from S.McNair (M.Stover kick), 14:26.

A—70,743.

SD		BAL
First downs	13	14
3rd down efficiency	2-13	4-11
Net yards	284	206
Rushing	150	56
Passing	134	150
Comp-att-int	13-23-1	17-30-2
Sacked—yards lost	1-11	2-8
Punts-average	5-53.8	7-48.0
Return yardage	144	138
Penalties-yards	10-77	4-30
Fumbles-lost	3-0	2-1
Time of possession	33:42	26:18

INDIVIDUAL STATISTICS

Rushing

      SD: L.Tomlinson 27-98, M.Turner 7-46, L.Neal 5-13, P.Rivers 1-0, M.Scifres 1-(-7).

      BAL: J.Lewis 15-34, Mu.Smith 2-14, S.McNair 2-11, M.Anderson 1-0, M.Clayton 1-(-3).

Passing

      SD: P.Rivers 13-22-1-145, M.Scifres 0-1-0-0.

      BAL: S.McNair 17-30-2-158.

Receiving

      SD: A.Gates 4-41, E.Parker 4-37, M.Floyd 1-31, L.Neal 1-18, L.Tomlinson 1-7, V.Jackson 1-6, B.Manumaleuna 1-5.

      BAL: T.Heap 4-60, M.Clayton 4-37, D.Mason 4-37, D.Wilcox 3-17, D.Williams 1-6, Mu.Smith 1-1.

Missed field goals

      SD: N.Kaeding 40.

Chapter 8: Fantasy Football and Other Fan Favorites

half a page, and you'll know what happened in yesterday's games, as well as how all of your fantasy players did.

But what if you want to find out more about a game? Ask a parent if you can go online to *www.nfl.com*. Click on "Game Book," found on the Game Center or box score pages, to get the full multipage game summary that is passed out to reporters after the game. You'll see the starting lineups, a summary of every play (including who made each tackle), drive charts, and even more statistics than are in the box score. If you couldn't see a game, the Game Book is the next best way to find out everything that happened.

Football Video Games

You can watch many different levels of football, from backyard touch football to NFL football. Guess what?

Fans Have Fun

Football fans really get into cheering on their team! Can you find your way from START to END through the crazy crowd?

The EVERYTHING KIDS' Football Book

The same is true of football video games.

Madden NFL

The game that everyone, even people who don't play video games, has heard about is Madden NFL. Since 2005, this has been the only video game that uses authentic NFL players, jerseys, coaches, and stadiums. Each year a new game, updated with current rosters and new features, is released. Each game is named a year ahead. For example, Madden NFL 2009 will be released in August 2008 and will use player statistics from 2007.

The graphics and sounds make this game seem real. Every uniform and stadium is shown accurately. Even the individual players are correctly simulated. Each player is rated from 1–100 on his skills and characteristics, such as speed, awareness, and strength. As you play the game, you hear John Madden and Al Michaels announcing, and it sounds just like a Sunday Night Football broadcast.

Madden NFL includes numerous special features and modes. You can pretend to be an owner by signing players, building stadiums, and hiring and firing coaches. In superstar mode you can pretend to be a rookie in the NFL and build yourself into a superstar over several seasons through great play and intelligent off-field decisions. You can play against the computer, against a friend, or even in online tournaments. Each year at the Super Bowl, actual NFL players play in a Madden NFL tournament against one another. Alex Smith, the 49ers quarterback, won that tournament in both 2006 and 2007.

All-Pro Football

The chief competitor to the Madden game is All-Pro Football by 2K Sports. The NFL does not allow All-Pro Football to use current players, teams, or anything about the NFL. So All-Pro has created a fictional league that's

The Madden Curse

Since 1999, Madden NFL comes in a box decorated with a picture of a great NFL player. The funny thing is, almost every season the player on the box seems to get hurt or to have a bad season. For the 2008 game, LaDainian Tomlinson was asked to be the player on the box, but he refused. Do you think he might have been afraid of the curse?

Backyard Football
Backyard Football has NFL uniforms, plays, and, of course, the
players—as kids! Not everyone in
the NFL is featured in this game,
but you can also custom design
your own players or choose from
the Backyard Gang.

similar to the NFL. The players are famous former NFL
players, many of whom are in the hall of fame. While
Madden has more features than many people can handle,
All-Pro's strength is its game play and strategy. Rather
than just picking the NFL team that you know is already
good, in All-Pro you have to tweak your roster to figure out
the best combination of all of the available great players.
Then, in the game, your ability to choose the correct play
call on offense and defense, as well as your ability to move
your players around, will determine how good you are.

NCAA Football

If you're more of a college football fan, then you can
get NCAA Football by EA Sports. This game is quite similar to Madden NFL in some of its features and game
play. In fact, you can create a superstar in NCAA Football and then continue his career in Madden NFL. All of
the college stadiums, uniforms, and coaches are authen-
tically shown. The players are not named because of
NCAA rules. But since the game's players look like real
players, wear the same numbers as real players, and
have the same moves as real players, you can figure
out who's who. In fact, you can even enter the players'
names in the game once you figure out who they are.

The Pro Football Hall of Fame

If you're a fan of the NFL, you will love a trip to the
hall of fame in Canton, Ohio. Even though the players
and teams that you'll see there probably played before
you started following football, you'll still enjoy learning
firsthand about some of the football history that you've
heard about.

What's in There?

When you enter the building, you'll see an enormous
room with a domed roof. In the middle is a life-sized
statue of Jim Thorpe. In the galleries around the statue

are some of the hall's most historically interesting displays, including:

- The shoe used to kick the longest field goal ever
- Jim Brown's helmet
- Walter Peyton's game uniform from when he broke the all-time rushing record
- Y.A. Tittle's old-style helmet that was cracked in half during a game
- An enormous knee brace worn by Joe Namath

The other members of the hall of fame don't get full life-sized statues, but they do all get bronze busts of their heads. One large room contains all of these busts, hundreds of faces staring out at the fans. In addition to the busts of the inductees, the hall contains displays celebrating great players of the past and present. These displays may show a game uniform, a photo of a player in action, or a plaque summarizing his accomplishments. Many of the player displays are grouped by team, so if you're a fan of one particular team, you can see its players all at once.

Aside from the busts and the descriptions of the players in the hall, the hall has a display of equipment worn by pro football players throughout history. You'll be amazed at the leather helmets without facemasks, the old-style shoulder pads, and the strange looking balls that were used way back in the 1920s. There are also the actual jerseys worn by players when important events happened. For example, you can see the uniform LaDainian Tomlinson wore when he set the NFL's season touchdown record in 2007. The hall collects the actual footballs used in historic games and stores them in a huge room in shoeboxes on shelves. Perhaps a few of these will be on display when you go!

How Are the Hall of Fame Players Chosen?

Hall of fame players are chosen by a selection committee. Each team sends one representative to this committee. Usually this is the reporter from the local newspaper who follows the team. Throughout the year, the selectors talk by e-mail and vote in order to create a ballot of seventeen hall of fame candidates for the year.

On the day before the Super Bowl, the whole committee meets to talk about that year's candidates. One person presents an argument for each of the possible hall of famers. Once the discussion is over, the selectors vote. The players with the most support become members of the hall of fame. Each year, the selectors are required to choose at least three new hall of famers, but they can't choose more than six.

The actual ceremony that makes someone a member of the hall of fame happens in July in Canton. The player is shown his bust, he's given a gold jacket, and he gets to make a speech to the crowd. Lots of fans attend these ceremonies, especially fans who went to games when the hall of famer was on the field. The induction ceremonies are televised, so you can watch without making the long trip to Canton.

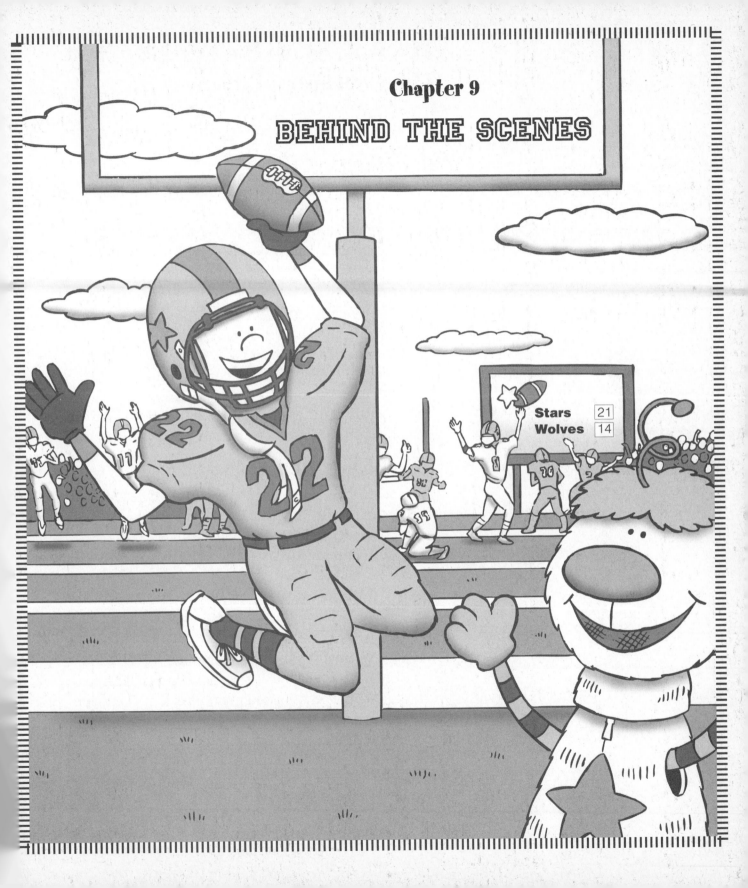

Chapter 9
BEHIND THE SCENES

Good Programs Have Good Assistants

The legendary Joe Paterno has been Penn State's head coach since 1966. Why has Joe—and the Penn State program—been so unbelievably successful? Well, among other reasons, Joe has a staff of outstanding assistants. If you go to a clinic or a camp there, you'll see that these folks might as well be called professors of football. These assistants haven't been at Penn State as long as Joe has, but they've averaged seventeen years on staff, including three assistants who have each coached with Joe for more than twenty years.

The Bosses on the Practice Field: The Coaching Staff

The head coach, especially the head coach of a major college or NFL team, is hardly behind the scenes. In fact, many big time head coaches host a weekly television show! Even high school head coaches are well known near-celebrities in their communities. The assistant coaches and the coaches of the lower-level high school teams, though, are not household names. These folks work hard too, but many people aside from the players likely do not know who they are or what they do.

College and Professional Assistant Coaches

Assistant coaches at the college and NFL level are career coaches, for the most part. They have decided that they want to learn how to be a big-time coach, often (but not always) with the goal of becoming a head coach somewhere. Coaching is these folks' full-time job. Most assistants are position coaches, with one person in charge of linebackers, another for defensive backs, and so on. An assistant's role is to relate personally to each player they're in charge of and to help those players develop their skills. In season, assistant coaches must understand each game plan, then figure out how to teach their players to execute that plan. If an effective football team consists of lots of different units working together, then the assistant coaches are the ones who train each individual unit.

High School Assistant Coaches

At the high school level, most assistants are teachers at the school. At first, you may think it a bit strange to have teachers as football coaches, especially if they teach something like physics or art. But it's not these teachers' academic knowledge that is useful on the football field but rather their teaching ability. Coaching, after all, is teaching: explaining techniques, motivating, helping players to learn new and sometimes difficult approaches. Coaching is not a high school assistant's full-time job. But then football is not a high school player's full-time job either. The players often develop an improved appreciation for their coaches' classes. They may not have enjoyed chemistry class before, but if the offensive line coach is also the chemistry teacher, they might find the subject more manageable.

Who Makes You Look Good: The Equipment Manager

The equipment manager is one of the most important of the support staff during the game. If someone's helmet breaks, he simply can't play unless someone, usually the equipment manager, fixes it. The equipment manager is also in charge of making sure every player's uniform is ready to go on game day.

Uniforms

Football is an all-weather outdoor sport. After a game, those great-looking uniforms become covered with grass stains, mud, and sweat. The equipment manager's main job is to get the uniforms clean for the next game. That's no mean task considering the average team has seventy to 100 sets of jerseys, pants, socks, and so on. Holes in jerseys have to be sewn back together. The uniforms go through the wash seven or eight times and are treated in between to help remove stains. When they're finally done, each complete uniform is assembled and hung in the correct player's locker. And there's more . . . much, much more. So much more, in fact, that a major college or NFL program has as many as ten to twenty people working under the supervision of the head equipment manager.

While the laundry from last week's game is in the machines, the equipment managers get ready for the week's practices. Each team's specific routine is different, but the main idea is the same for all: get each player the correct practice jersey. This is more complicated than you might think. The team can't all look the same for practice because they have to have different colored jerseys for offense and defense. Some teams have even more different outfits. Perhaps the starters and reserves wear different colors too. The coaches might also have special requests. For example, if the next opponent wears green and has a really good linebacker who wears the number fifty, the coaches might ask for one of their own scout team linebackers to wear a green number fifty jersey in practice. The equipment managers have to sort out the practice jerseys, giving the correct one to each player, then they have to have all the rest of the players' equipment ready, including helmets, pads, and shoes.

Heavy Lifting

While laundry and practice preparation are going on, the staff is still unpacking stuff from the previous week's game, cleaning, organizing, and repacking for the next week's game. During a game, things gets damaged, broken, and lost. The equipment manager must be able to replace any piece of equipment instantly. That takes organization and planning. The team brings extra shoes, cleats, pants, mouthpieces, pads, and pretty much anything needed to keep every player available for the whole game. It takes a good part of a week's work to get all of this spare stuff in the right place, ready for travel to the game site.

Two or three days before an away game, the entire staff loads everything onto a huge truck. This truck drives to the game, arriving well before the team. The equipment managers themselves fly with the team, but they don't get to go right to the team hotel. They have to meet the truck and unload all of the equipment onto the sideline before they can rest.

Fancy Footwork

Break the letter and number equations to find the silly answer to the riddle.

Why did the official kick Cinderella out of the game?

>FWEEP<

A+4
I-1
P+3
X+1   G-2
B-1   F+2
I-4   T+3   V-2
R+1   D-3
V-1   J+3   J+2
D-3   M+1   L+3   N-2
A+2   E-4   S-1   D-3
G-2   P+2   D+2   A+1
G-5

Respecting the Student Managers

Unfortunately, sometimes there are players who don't understand how important and hard working the managers are. A good coach will not allow this behavior. Most coaches lecture the team at the beginning of the season about how to treat the managers respectfully. At the end of the year, the coaches make sure that the managers get the same kind of honors as the players do.

The head equipment manager can work eighty-hour weeks during the season. That's crazy—forty hours per week is the standard for most workers! Taking care of a team's stuff is long, hard work, but it all pays off on game day.

Team Managers

Think about all the small jobs that need to be done to help out a football team. There are a lot of these. Someone needs to fill up water bottles before practice and during practice, then the water bottles need to be cleaned up and put away. What about the footballs themselves? Someone has to take charge of giving out balls to various coaches and players who need them for practice, then collecting them after practice, finding any that got thrown into the bushes, and putting them away where they belong.

Managers are critical to the team's success, so a good coaching staff will bend over backward to let them know their importance. Managers pack up for away games with the rest of the equipment staff. They prowl the sideline on game day, filling whatever role is needed. Some will fetch and (on bad weather days) clean the game balls.

So You Want to Be a Manager?

Perhaps the best way for a young person to get involved with a football team is as a manager. High school teams have occasionally used managers as young as nine or ten. Even if you don't know anyone on the team, show up to practice a few times just to watch. Look carefully at what goes on and figure out something you could do to make practice go smoother for everyone. For example, maybe one of the coaches is having trouble carrying around his clipboard and running a drill at the same time. Before practice one day, go up to the coach and ask him if you could carry the clipboard for him.

Start small, asking to do one or two specific things. During practice, try to be as quiet and useful as you can. If you're a hard worker who learns how the team operates, you'll be surprised how quickly you will be asked to take on more jobs. The coaches will come to rely on you to take care of things, so you'll be asked to come to the games to work. Ta-da—you're a student manager!

OW! The Athletic Trainer

Football is a hard-hitting game. After a game or a hard practice, every player, even the best-conditioned athlete, feels sore. Isn't it great that the athletic trainer is there, waiting to help you feel better?

The Athletic Trainer's Job

Most high school athletic programs have an athletic trainer who works with athletes in all their sports. Colleges and NFL football teams employ four or even five trainers for their roster of sixty to ninety players. These trainers are all an integral part of the team. During the seven months of the season, these dedicated folks work seven days a week. They tape ankles and otherwise prepare every player for every practice. They help supervise rehabilitation. After practice, trainers help players ice, stretch, and otherwise assist their bodies start the recovery process so they'll be ready for the next practice.

Major injuries in football are, in fact, reasonably rare. Studies show that soccer players are considerably more likely to suffer serious injuries than football players. Why? One reason for the low injury rate is that football teams actively work to prevent injury. The athletic trainers supervise the stretching and taping that is an important part of injury prevention. Trainers also attend daily to all the nagging, minor soreness and strains that could become major injuries without treatment. And, of course, state-of-the-art protective equipment absorbs most of the hard hits.

NFL trainers travel with the team the day before a game. At the team hotel, the training staff takes over a big conference room to use as a training room. On game day, the trainers work nonstop. They open up their hotel training room as early as they wake up. Then they move all of their equipment to the game site. Several hours before the game, players begin to show up for pregame preparation. The trainers will spend at least five minutes per player taping ankles, stretching out tight muscles, covering protective casts, and making sure that every player's body is ready by game time.

During the game, the trainers spread out on the sideline with the team. They are instantly ready to deal with injuries, both major and minor. They (along with the team doctor) tell the coach which injured players can get back in the game and who needs to sit out. Game time is what the trainers live for. Even though they're not playing, they get the same rush of excitement as the players do because 70,000 fans are screaming for the team to win, and the trainers are part of that team.

The trainer's job never ends. Even on the plane ride home, trainers are giving out ice packs and making sure injured players are positioned correctly. Then, after everyone else has gone home, the trainers stick around for an extra hour or so with injured players to get treatment started right away.

The EVERYTHING KIDS' Football Book

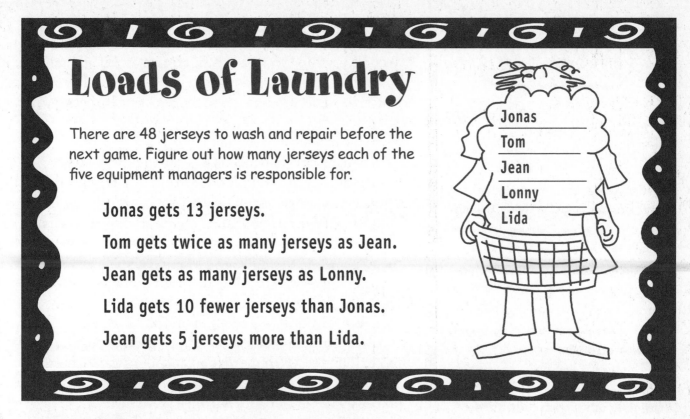

Loads of Laundry

There are 48 jerseys to wash and repair before the next game. Figure out how many jerseys each of the five equipment managers is responsible for.

Jonas gets 13 jerseys.

Tom gets twice as many jerseys as Jean.

Jean gets as many jerseys as Lonny.

Lida gets 10 fewer jerseys than Jonas.

Jean gets 5 jerseys more than Lida.

Jonas _____
Tom _____
Jean _____
Lonny _____
Lida _____

So You Want to Be an Athletic Trainer?

First, you have to get a college degree. Ideally, you'd major in the physical or biological sciences, but there are also programs specifically in health, fitness, and exercise science. You can earn a masters or professional degree in athletic training and take some tests to become an officially certified trainer. Then you're ready to apply for a job. It's an intense job, but it's an awesome one too.

Keeping a Clean Game: The Officials

There is a job you can do every weekend. You'll have to spend hours ahead of time getting ready: going to meetings, studying, and traveling. You have to pass a test to be allowed to do the job. When it's time to start, you'll be expected to sprint a total of several miles to keep up with people who are faster than you. You can expect to

FUN FACT

get knocked down occasionally by giants wearing armor. Everyone—maybe thousands of people—will complain about everything you do. They'll scream at you and call you names, even if you do a good job. When it's all over, you'll get paid. Woo-hoo! Go to the bookstore to spend your paycheck, and you'll be able to buy maybe two books. Such is the life of a football official.

Though they do hard work, football officials truly love what they are doing. For one thing, they know how critical they are to the game. Can you imagine a game without officials? That wouldn't work. Though fans and coaches will yell at them, most of them respect the tremendous effort that officials put into calling every game.

The people who officiate do so for many reasons. Many are former athletes who are too old to play anymore but who still love football and want to stay involved. Some might not have been good enough to play football but are extremely good at calling the game. Officials must be just as focused in their minds and their bodies as the players are during a game.

Most importantly, despite the craziness, officiating football can be fun. How many times have you watched a game on TV and wished you could be part of the action?

How to Become an Official

Start by finding a local officiating association. Find one on the Internet or talk to the referee before a game at a nearby high school. In most areas, officials join an association and then the association assigns them to local games. The higher-level games, and especially the playoff games, go to the best and most experienced people.

Talk to the person in charge. Depending on the sport and the locality, there are different requirements to meet before you're allowed to work games. You're almost definitely too young to work a game right now. But you're not too young to learn the rules and what are called the mechanics—where to go on the field, what to look for, and how to make a call. Let the people in the association give you advice on where to start.

The EVERYTHING KIDS' Football Book

Officiating Positions

Football officials work in teams. A junior varsity game might have four officials. The NFL and most college conferences use seven officials on a team. Every member of the team has a different job to do.

- The referee is the crew chief, supervising all the officials on the team. During the game, the referee stands behind the offense and is primarily responsible for watching the quarterback. He announces penalties to the coaches and the spectators.
- The umpire stands directly behind the defensive line. His job is to watch the blockers to make sure no one is holding. He also gets the ball ready for the next play.
- The head linesman and the line judge stand on the sideline, right on the line of scrimmage. They look to see that the play starts correctly, then they are responsible for any action near the sideline. The head linesman runs the chain crew, making sure they can measure for a first down if necessary.
- The field judge, side judge, and back judge start each play way behind the defense. They watch out for pass interference. They take over watching the action when a play goes for long yardage. Some leagues, especially in high school, only use a field judge, not a side or back judge.

Football GREAT

Famous Referees

Ed Hochuli, a lawyer from Wisconsin, has worked in the NFL for more than seventeen years. Mike Carey, from San Diego, holds the longest current streak of consecutive postseason assignments, though he has not yet worked a Super Bowl. Carey and Hochuli are the referees featured in the Madden NFL video games. They are both known for their clear explanations of penalties over the stadium microphone.

Appendix A

FOOTBALL FACTS AND RECORDS

The records football players hold help fans understand just how good they were. Here are some of the important NFL individual career records:

Most Rushing Yards

Emmitt Smith	Cowboys, Cardinals	18,355
Walter Payton	Bears	16,726
Barry Sanders	Lions	15,269

Most Passing Yards

Brett Favre	Packers, Falcons	61,655
Dan Marino	Dolphins	61,361
John Elway	Broncos	51,475

Most Receiving Yards

Jerry Rice	49ers, Raiders, Seahawks	22,895
Tim Brown	Raiders, Buccaneers	14,934

Most Touchdowns Scored

Jerry Rice	49ers, Raiders, Seahawks	208
Emmitt Smith	Cowboys, Cardinals	175
Marcus Allen	Raiders, Chiefs	145

Most Points Scored

Morten Anderson	Saints, Falcons, and others	2,445
Gary Anderson	Steelers, Vikings, and others	2,434
George Blanda	Bears, Oilers, Raiders	2,002

The EVERYTHING KIDS' Football Book

NFL Team Records

While individuals are important, football is a team game. Here are some NFL team records:

Most Super Bowl Victories

Steelers, Cowboys, 49ers	5

Most Super Bowls Played

Cowboys	8
Broncos, Steelers	6

Most Seasons in the Playoffs

Cowboys, Giants	28
Rams	27
Browns, Vikings	24

Most NFL Championships

Packers	12
Bears	9
Giants	6

College Team Records

It's tough to find meaningful college football records. Since there's not a playoff, each year might have several national champions. Individual statistics don't mean a lot either, since some teams schedule easy games designed just to get players more yards gained. But here are some notable college team records:

Most National Championships

Notre Dame	13
Southern California, Michigan, Alabama	11
Oklahoma	9

Most Big Ten Championships

Michigan	42

| Ohio State | 32 |
| Minnesota | 18 |

Most Pac 10 Championships

Southern California	37
UCLA (University of California, Los Angeles)	17
Washington	15

Most SEC Championships

Alabama	21
Tennessee	13
Georgia	12

Most Rose Bowl Victories

Southern California	23
Michigan	8
Washington	6

Most Orange Bowl Victories

Oklahoma	12
Nebraska	8
Miami	6

The Heisman Trophy

The Heisman is awarded each year to an outstanding college football player. Football writers and broadcasters vote for the winner. In 2007, Florida's Tim Tebow won the award, making him the only player to receive the honor in only his sophomore year.

Most Heisman Trophies

| Archie Griffin | Ohio State | 2 |

Heisman Trophy winners who also made the Pro Football Hall of Fame include:

- Doak Walker, Southern Methodist
- Paul Hornung, Notre Dame
- Roger Staubach, Navy
- Tony Dorsett, Pittsburgh
- Earl Campbell, Texas
- Marcus Allen, Southern California
- Barry Sanders, Oklahoma State

Heisman trophy winners who are playing in the NFL as of the 2007 season include:

- Troy Smith, Ohio State—a backup quarterback for the Ravens in 2007
- Reggie Bush, Southern California—a running back for the Saints since 2006
- Matt Leinart, Southern California—the Cardinals' starting quarterback since mid-2006
- Carson Palmer, Southern California—the Bengals' starting quarterback since 2004
- Ron Dayne, Wisconsin—running back for the Giants, Broncos, and Texans
- Charles Woodson, Michigan—cornerback for the Raiders and the Packers

GLOSSARY

ATHLETIC SCHOLARSHIP:
Money given to a college athlete to pay for all living expenses.

BALL SECURITY:
Holding on to the ball correctly so as not to fumble.

BLACKOUT:
If an NFL game is not sold out three days ahead of time, the game cannot be shown on TV in the home team's city.

BLITZ:
When more than four defensive players rush the quarterback.

BYE:
A week when a team doesn't play a game. NFL teams get one bye each season.

CHAIN GANG:
The people who carry a chain to indicate the line for the next first down.

COFFIN CORNER:
A punt that goes out of bounds near (but not in) the end zone.

COMMISSIONER:
The person in charge of a league. The commissioner of the NFL is Roger Goodell. A fantasy league also appoints a commissioner.

CONTAIN:
The defensive line tries to keep, or contain, the quarterback in the pocket.

CROSSING ROUTES:
When receivers run routes with crossing paths, designed to confuse a zone defense.

DEFENSE:
The part of a football team that tries to stop the offense from scoring.

DRAW PLAY:
A running play that starts after the defense thinks it's a passing play.

ELIGIBLE RECEIVER:
Anyone who is allowed to catch a pass. This usually includes everyone except the five offensive linemen.

FLEA FLICKER:
A trick play. The running back is handed the ball and starts to run but throws the ball back to the quarterback for a long pass.

HOLDING:
Unless he's trying to tackle the ballcarrier, no one is allowed to grab, hug, or tackle. Holding results in a ten-yard penalty.

HOMECOMING:
The game when the school's graduates come back to watch and celebrate.

HOME-FIELD ADVANTAGE:
For a lot of reasons, the home team wins about 60 percent of all NFL games.

HOT ROUTE:
A route run by a receiver for when the defense blitzes.

INDEPENDENTS:
College football teams that do not belong to a conference.

The **EVERYTHING KIDS'** Football Book

LATERAL:

A backward pass. Any player can throw a lateral at any time.

LUXURY BOX:

A fancy room in a football stadium with food, drinks, and nice furniture.

MERGER, THE:

In 1970, the American Football League and the National Football League came together to form a single NFL.

NFL:

These initials stand for National Football League. This is the most successful professional sports league in the world.

OFFENSE:

The part of a football team that controls the ball and tries to score.

ON AN ISLAND:

When a cornerback has to cover a receiver man-to-man without help.

PASS INTERFERENCE:

A penalty called when the defensive player hits a receiver while a pass is in the air.

PLAY:

A play starts when the center snaps the ball; a play ends when the ballcarrier is tackled or goes out of bounds.

POCKET:

The area where the quarterback stands to throw a pass.

REDSHIRT:

Sitting out for a year to gain an extra year of eligibility for a college football player.

SACK:

When the quarterback wants to pass but is tackled behind the line of scrimmage.

SCREEN PASS:

A short pass designed to fool the defense.

TOUCHBACK:

A kick or a punt that enters the end zone, allowing the offense to take possession on the twenty-yard line.

SINGLE WING:

A formation, rarely used today, with lots of tight linemen to help run the football.

SNAP COUNT.

The number of "Hut!"s that the quarterback says before the snap.

T FORMATION:

An offensive formation that puts the quarterback under center with three running backs behind the quarterback.

TACKLE:

Making the ballcarrier fall to the ground. The offensive linemen who line up outside the guards. The defensive linemen who line up closest to the ball.

TAILGATING:

Having a cookout or a party in the parking lot before a football game.

TWO-A-DAYS:

Preseason practices that happen twice a day.

WEST COAST OFFENSE:

A passing offense that features short passing routes.

WILD CARD:

A team that makes the playoffs but didn't win its division.

YAC:

Stands for yards after catch, the yardage that a receiver gains after he catches the ball.

Appendix B: Glossary

Appendix C
PUZZLE ANSWERS

Find the Flag • page 3

Way to Play • page 13

I		P	L	A	Y		T	W	O
P	O	S	I	T	I	O	N	S	-
F	I	R	S	T		I	'	M	
C	R	O	U	C	H	E	D		
D	O	W	N	,		T	H	E	N
I	'	M		U	P		A	N	D
R	U	N	N	I	N	G	!		

Woofball • page 9

A GOLDEN RECEIVER!

Lost Player • page 19

Why did the football coach shake the vending machine?

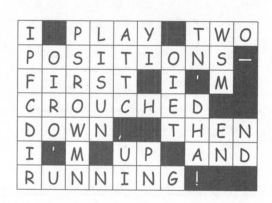

| 1 H | 2 E | | 3 W | 4 A | 5 N | 6 T | 7 E | 8 D | | 9 H | 10 I | 11 S |
| 12 Q | 13 U | 14 A | 15 R | 16 T | 17 E | 18 R | | 19 B | 20 A | 21 C | 22 K | ! |

Where you wear a glove
H A N D
9 20 5 8

Opposite of loud
Q U I E T
12 13 10 2 6

Opposite of dry
W E T
3 7 16

Piece of equipment
that stops a car
B R A K E
19 15 14 22 17

What happens when
a car doesn't stop
C R A S H
21 18 4 11 1

The EVERYTHING KIDS' Football Book

Find the Football • page 22

Fractured Football • page 33

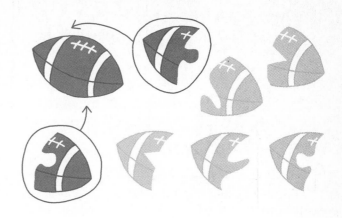

Brush Up • page 24

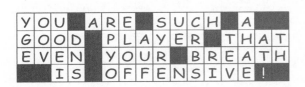

YOU ARE SUCH A GOOD PLAYER THAT EVEN YOUR BREATH IS OFFENSIVE!

Football Fill In • pages 38-39

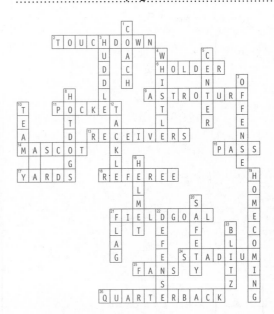

Perfect Play • page 27

Super Sized • page 44

The one with the biggest head!

Appendix C: Puzzle Answers

Go Team! · page 53

RAH, RAH, RAH!
SKI-U-MAH,
HOO-RAH!
HOO-RAH!
VARSITY!
VARSITY!
VARSITY,
MINN-E-SO-TAH!

"Ski-U-Mah" is pronounced SKY-YOU-MAH. "Ski" is a Native American battle cry meaning "victory." "U-Mah" represents the <u>U</u>niversity of <u>M</u>innesota.

What's in a Name? · page 55

The most popular mascots are:

EAGLES   BULLDOGS   TIGERS   LIONS

Some more unusual mascots are:

PENGUINS   KANGAROOS   OWLS   BLUE HENS

Twin Teammates · page 59

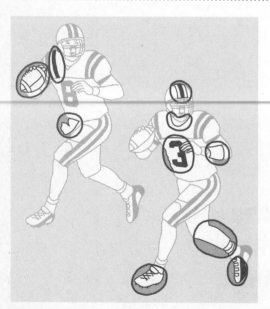

Where's the Player? · page 60

What is the difference between a football player and a duck?

. . . .

You'll find one in a huddle, and the other in a puddle!

Pep Rally · page 64

lunch wrappers and empty lunch bag
T R A <u>S</u> H

mistake in Drivers' Ed.
C R A <u>S</u> H

important to have in chorus
B <u>R</u> E A <u>T</u> H

art project with dried flowers
<u>W</u> R E A <u>T</u> H

what boring teachers do
P <u>R</u> E A C <u>H</u>

activity in math class
G <u>R</u> A P <u>H</u>

after-school fundraiser
C A <u>R</u> <u>W</u> A <u>S</u> H

The Silly Anser Is . . . · page 68

IF	~~TENNIS~~	TWO	~~DISC~~
~~ON~~	FLIES	ARE	~~BASKETBALL~~
~~KITCHEN~~	~~CLOSET~~	~~AIR~~	~~BAT~~
IN	~~VOLLEYBALL~~	THE	~~WEBSTER~~
~~SPIDERS~~	KITCHEN	~~HAMMER~~	WHICH
~~AT~~	ONE	~~RUDDERS~~	~~JAR~~
IS	~~LID~~	THE	~~PING PONG~~
~~BADMINTON~~	FOOTBALL	~~AX~~	PLAYER

Hide the Football · page 73

1. Is the game on one di<u>sc or e</u>leven cassettes?

2. We won! Hear <u>us "</u>Hooray!"

3. The champ <u>lay</u> winded in the end zone.

4. The quarterback <u>spun</u>, then threw the ball.

5. Tired players <u>nap</u> before a big game.

6. Don't pani<u>c! Lock</u> the stadium door!

7. All <u>I</u> need is to move the ball four more yards!

8. Losing team<u>s weep</u> in private.

9. All of Ray <u>Spigs' kin</u> came to watch him play!

10. Drinking iced <u>tea</u> makes players less thirsty.

The EVERYTHING KIDS' Football Book